*Vancouver Magazine's
Pocket Restaurant Guide*

Vancouver Magazine's Pocket Restaurant Guide

Brad Ovenell-Carter
and Scott Mowbray

WHITECAP BOOKS

Vancouver/Toronto

Copyright © 1992 by Telemedia Communications Inc.

Whitecap Books
Vancouver/Toronto

All rights reserved. No part of this publication may be reproduced, stored in a retrieval system, or transmitted, in any form or by any means, electronic, mechanical, photocopying, recording or otherwise, without the prior written permission of the publisher.

Edited by Pat Crowe
Cover design by Warren Clark
Interior design by Carolyn Deby

Typeset at Vancouver Desktop Publishing, Vancouver
Printed and bound in Canada by Friesen Printers, Altona, Manitoba

Canadian Cataloguing in Publication Data

Ovenell-Carter, Brad.
  Vancouver magazine's pocket restaurant guide

  Includes index.
  ISBN 1-55110-041-X

  1. Restaurants, lunch rooms, etc.—British Columbia—Vancouver—Guidebooks. I. Mowbray, Scott. II. Title.
TX907.5.C22V354 1992   647.95711'33   C92-091535-3

*Cet ouvrage a été composé
par Atlant'Communication
aux Sables-d'Olonne (Vendée)*

*Impression réalisée par
Liberduplex*

*pour le compte des Éditions Archipoche
en mars 2008*

*Imprimé en Espagne
N° d'édition : 65
Dépôt légal : mai 2008*

48. « La royauté est un crime de lèse-humanité ! »   519
49. Midi et quart, place de la Révolution   527
Postface   535

CONTENTS

Introduction ix

Chinese

Dynasty 2
Fortune House 4
Kirin 6

Bodai 7
Chilli House 8
Hon's 9
Landmark Hot Pot . . 9
Moutai Mandarin . . 10
Park Lock 10
Pink Pearl 11

European

Chartwell 14
Adega 15
Chesa 16
CinCin 16
Santos Tapas 17
Vassilis 17
William Tell 18

French

Cafe de Paris 22
Le Coq D'Or 22
Le Crocodile 24

Chez Thierry 25
La Toque Blanche . . 26
Le Gavroche 26
Le Club 28

Hamburgers

Milestones 30

Hamburger Mary's . . 30
Red Robin 31

Indian/African/ Lebanese

Ashiana 34
Natraj 34
Rubina Tandoori . . . 35

Dar Lebanon 36
Elissar 37
Nyala 37
Raga 38

Italian

Il Barino 40
Il Giardino 41
Villa Del Lupo 42

Bianco Nero 43
Cafe Il Nido 44
Napoli Restaurant . 45
Piccolo Mondo . . . 45
Saltimbocca 46
Salute 47
Settebello 47
Splendido 48
Umberto Al Porto . 49
Zefferelli's 50
Zeppo's Trattoria . . 50

Japanese

Hoshi 54
Raku 55
Tojo's 56

Aki 57
Ezogiku Noodle Cafe 58
Kitto 58
Koko 59
Kyocha Ya 59
Noodle Express . . 60

Mexican

El Mariachi 62

Cha Cha Cha 63
Las Margaritas 63
Pepitas 64

North American

Bishop's 66
Joe Fortes 67
Raintree 67

Alma Street Cafe . . 68
Barbara-Jo's 69
Beach Side Cafe . . . 69
Delilah's 71
Earl's 72
English Bay Cafe . . 73
Five Sails 73
Harpo's 74
Mescalero 74
Mocha Cafe 75
Monterey 75
Sophie's Cosmic Cafe 76

Pizza

Flying Wedge 78
Lombardo's 78
Passionate Pizza . . 79

Did's Pizza 79
Pizza Rico's 80
Slice of Gourmet . . 80

Seafood

The Cannery 84
The Amorous Oyster 84

Bud's Halibut and
  Chips 85
The Only Seafood
  Cafe 85
Pajo's 86
Salmon House on the
  Hill 86

Southeast Asian

Sawasdee 88
Phnom Penh 88
Viet Nam Cuisine . . 89

Arirang House . . . 90
Bangkok House . . . 91
Montri's 91
Nonya Baba 92
Palayok 92
Pho Hoang 93
Pho Van 93
Rumah Bali 94
Tea and Silk 94

Alphabetical Index 97
Index by Area 99
Index by Price . . . 101

Introduction

As Vancouver has become a world-class city, its restaurants have grown apace, so that now residents and tourists alike can enjoy a phenomenal range of international cuisine, prepared with the freshest ingredients by top-notch chefs, all in the area of a few square kilometers.

This book reflects the best of our dining scene—the top 100 restaurants—as selected by two writers who know Vancouver food better than anyone I can think of. Brad Ovenell-Carter is currently *Vancouver* magazine's food editor. He brings to his journalism fifteen years of experience in the food-service industry—as a waiter, a chef, and as a hotel and restaurant manager. He regularly shares his passion for food and wine with the listeners of CBC Radio's "Early Edition." Scott Mowbray was food editor of *Western Living* magazine before becoming editor of *Vancouver* magazine, while continuing to write its Diner column; for five years, he was the food and restaurant critic for CBC Radio's "The Afternoon Show," and, having once written an award-winning series of articles on nutrition for *Western Living* and *Ontario Living* magazines, he recently authored *The Food Fight: Truth, Myth and the Food-Health Connection* (Random House).

A few ground rules:

Like Ovenell-Carter's and Mowbray's magazine pieces, these reviews are based on anonymous visits to each restaurant. We paid our own tab. Judgments have been made carefully but, of course, subjectively. Prices denoted at the end of each review are estimates—unless for instance we're talking about a by-the-slice pizza joint—for a three-course meal for two, without wine. You'll notice that some of the menus reflect seasonal variety (summer dishes, winter dishes, and so on); we've done this to provide a sense of a restaurant's versatility at various times of the year. Bear in mind that chefs come and go, and that menus are frequently revamped. All that said, we've done everything possible to be accurate at press time.

Finally, each cuisine in this book begins with two or three substantial reviews; these are places we would highly recommend for a special occasion. But length isn't everything. Following these main reviews are a selection of shorter ones for restaurants that are often just as stellar; they may simply have a culinary emphasis or specialty that lends itself to concise description.

Bon appetit!

John T.D. Keyes
Editor, *Vancouver* magazine

Chinese

Dynasty
1133 W. Hastings St. 689-9211

There are a thousand things to learn in a Chinese restaurant. Pigeon brains—what little you can glean from a cracked pigeon skull—have a chalky, cream-cheese texture and intensely gamey taste. Snow frog cream is, indeed, something derived from snow frogs.

The menu at Dynasty in the jazzy Ramada Renaissance hotel is one of the most intriguing in this city. Snow frog cream aside, dish after dish is not only unexpected but sounds good: sautéed Chinese keeper's pork with sausage and spinach; diced whelk with chicken, shrimp and walnuts; deep-fried crispy chicken with essence of champagne; sliced teal with honey peas and pickled cabbage.

The style is Hong Kong fusion—"Cantonese cuisine with French service," according to their own press release—with hints of North American cooking trends and chef Lam Kam Shing's background in China, Hong Kong and Japan. Duck is combined in soup with Japanese noodles, for example, and lobster meets banana in a delicate spring roll. For good measure, the menu throws in Szechuan and Peking dishes. The room, too, is striking, with tables set among a forest of white pillars. The ceiling is a white jigsaw puzzle with black fissures cut between the pieces. Above some of the tables, wood scaffolding supports a network of low-voltage live wires and numerous trapeze-like tiny halogen spot lamps. A big curving wall of glass faces Hastings Street.

What was once missing from our Dynasty dinners was the combination of vegetable crunch, garden freshness, seafood sweetness and perfect execution that distinguishes the best Cantonese cooking. This has been corrected. Braised vegetables with bamboo pith are a benchmark dish in which individual flavors shine through a sauce of superior stock. The lobster-banana rolls were delightful. In another dish, the unctuous flavor of sautéed walnuts went perfectly with tender whelks, shrimp and asparagus in a smooth garlicky glaze. Other successes: pan-fried bean curd rolls with vegetables; and abalone with chopped mushrooms, greens and a mess of hair-thin seaweed. Expect good advice in planning your meal, and take advantage of the special menus celebrating the many festivals of regional China.

Dim sum—ordered á là carte at lunch—is especially good: fabulously tender squid in the mildest sort of Singapore-style satay sauce; barbecued pork in flaky pastry, like tiny pigs-in-blankets; deep-fried little pillows of shrimp and chives; fried crabmeat rolls that seem to contain a lining of *nori* (seaweed); the usual roundup of steamed dumplings are particularly succulent and juicy.

There is a much more extensive wine list than usually found at Chinese restaurants, including two wines from China, and there's a selection of teas. Food prices average *$90* for a dinner for four, *$35* for a two-person dim sum. *Licensed.*

Fortune House
5733 Cambie St. 266-7728

A close read of the menu turns up a lot that seems right for Vancouver's wet weather: braised pigeon with ginger; braised eggplant with chili sauce and pork; baked black cod with bean sauce; marinated spare ribs; braised shrimps with sea cucumber and shrimp eggs; steamed bean curd with cured ham and mushrooms; sticky rice with Chinese sausage and keeper's pork. These are dishes whose descriptions suggest solidity and heat, whose techniques—baking, braising, steaming, preserving—are good ones for food that friends can linger around.

Mind you, the room could be warmer. There's a sort of generic upmarket Chinese restaurant decor in town that this restaurant has in spades: a bland plushness of neutral tones and rich materials (etched glass, glossy lacquered chairs, brass and mirrors) in big rooms, brightly lit. Then again, it's understood that this rote richness of the surroundings, this mall-like ambience (the restaurant is in Oakridge mall, in fact), is all about the Chinese-restaurant customers' two abiding priorities: food and conviviality.

The Fortune House kitchen reveals a steadiness and concentration that put it above many in its class. Although refined in an upscale way, the food is usually not oversubtle. Textures are lovely, flavors fresh and forward. Seafood is not overdone. Braised dishes are juicy but not mushy. Sauces are thickened to an ideal turn. The food arrives hot, seconds from pot or oven or wok.

Especially good was deep-fried bean cake with

minced crab and shrimp which yielded crusty little packets of bean curd, soft and moist and hot within, each bite taking in bits of green onion and seafood. Sticky rice with Chinese sausage and keeper's pork is a mélange of chewy textures, the rice deeply browned and slightly oily, the tidbits of sausage and bacon-like pork lending bursts of sweetness and smokiness by turn. The sautéed scallops in white wine garlic sauce were large, sea-sweet and tender; the sauce was intensely garlicky but a very clear, light glaze nonetheless. Pork ribs with "deep-fried milk" were oddly appealing in their orange-red glaze, very sweet and tender and tasting of peanuts. The deep-fried milk (common enough in Chinese restaurants—little blobs of fried blancmange) was unusually sweet here, coconut-flavored and served, redundantly, with dipping sugar. You could eat this dish for dessert. Deep-fried squid with spicy salt produced a heap of deeply scored squid curlicues in a light batter with chopped chilies and salt.

Prices are reasonable for food this good: about *$20* per person for dinner, without liquor. They rise when you order traditional delicacies, of course, and the menu has plenty: braised shark's fin with crab meat for four, *$72*; bird's nest in almond juice, *$28* per person; double-boiled "Buddhist delicacies" soup, *$32* per person. *$45. Licensed.*

Kirin
1166 Alberni St. 682-8833
555 W. 12th Ave. 879-8038

The Kirin downtown (Alberni Street) is a big fancy Mandarin restaurant in an office tower. Despite its impressive decor, it can feel lobbyish. The Kirin Seafood (West 12th Avenue) has a rather grand bank of seafood tanks keeping your meal fresh, hardwood furniture, a well-appointed private room and a view of the city from the north side of the dining room. Both places have a split-level arrangement that breaks up what could be cavernous.

But you come here for the food, which can be very good, especially if you push the serving staff for more unusual dishes. The menu is long, as Mandarin menus will be, and presented in Chinese, English, and Japanese. Traditional dishes, especially those from Shanghai and Beijing, are very well done, albeit on the sweet side for Western palates. But this may be a stylistic choice: the people of those regions do prefer this richness in their food.

Appetizers, elaborately arranged, include ultra-thin, blanched geoduck dipped into an oniony soy mixture, very sweet dried fish, and deep-fried squid. There is also a combination plate with drunken chicken, silky-textured white cooked pork, and mung-bean skin.

Entrées move from the classic Peking duck, served with superb, chewy, almost doughy crêpes, to first-rate Dungeness crab with ginger and scallions. One of the tricks to ordering Chinese is to move quickly away from the "safe" dishes. Here, as in other Chinese restaurants, the staff—the servers and the cooks—seem to improve as you get daring. Try braised sea cucumber in prawn roe sauce. This is the definitive, melt-in-your-mouth dish with a round ham-enriched brown sauce—easily as good as you find in the mother country. Also excellent: the red-brick-colored deep-fried smoked duck that mixes rich, crisp, smoky, crunchy flavors and textures.

Of the two locations, dim sum is superior at Kirin Seafood. Of special note, the *hargou* (shrimp dumplings) are some of the best in the city—fat and succulent with whole large shrimps. The *nori* tofu (seaweed and tofu) rolls are a study in texture and taste like the sea.

Service is Hong Kong formal style, which means lots of earnest waiters. One caution: be firm in your ordering. The staff can be aggressive when selling such high-priced items as king crab and fresh eel.

The wine list is above average for Chinese restaurants. Kirin also stocks a few good-quality teas that are available on request; try *ti guan yin* or jasmine. *$65. Licensed.*

Bodai Vegetarian Restaurant
337 E. Hastings St. 682-2666

This restaurant features adventures with bean curd and wheat gluten in the Chinese Buddhist tradition: vegetarian "shrimp," "chicken tenderloin," "barbecued pork," "squid," "duck" and other mock meats, along with all kinds of vegetables, noodles and rice. Vegetarian shrimp are curled-up, pink-speckled lumps that have the texture of sautéed shrimp but not the flavor; they're served with mushrooms and roasted cashews. Vegetarian chicken is firm and lightly smoked. This food is much more than a curiosity; it tastes good and is lightly cooked; it's low-calorie and delicate—except for the deep-fried dishes, of course, which are among the best: packets of bean curd skin stuffed with seaweed or—delicious—mashed taro root. There is a dish of deep-fried sweet and sour walnuts, and the requisite "deep-fried milk." Deluxe *lo-hon* vegetables produces a wealth of braised mushrooms, including, unfortunately, the canned variety. Singapore fried rice noodles are standard issue but done with a judicious amount of oil, tasting of curry powder and star anise. The room is bright and modern. Go with a group and experiment. *$35. Licensed.*

Chilli House
611 East Broadway. 873-4688

The menu suggests another pedestrian Chinese/Southeast Asian hybrid, hole-in-the-wall restaurant, but the food is surprisingly well-made and of very good value. Fried cuttlefish with Chinese vegetables yields squid that tastes almost of the grill, with a light glaze and considerable garlic; the seafood fried rice has a peppery bite, and lots of perfectly cooked bits of seafood, including prawns, scallops and octopus. Chicken with lemon juice is battered, dry-fried but tender and served with a very pure-tasting, thickened lemon sauce. As for the decor . . . what decor? Service is cheerful. This is a good lunch spot if you're in the Broadway and Fraser area. *$18. Licensed.*

Hon's
108-268 Keefer St. 688-0871

Improved service; clean, bright, busy, but you seldom wait long for endless variations of wide or thin rice noodles, egg noodles served with or without lettuce, barbecued pork, shrimp balls and so on. A standby to order when choices overwhelm: rice noodles with boiled beef, wonton, and lettuce, plus shots of Hon's formidable rendering of chili oil to animate. *$10. Licensed.*

Landmark Hot Pot House
4023 Cambie St. 872-2868

The specialty is two-soup hot pot (with a peanut soup on one side and a broth on the other) into which the diner plunges elaborately prepared but raw foods ordered from an intriguing list that includes live prawns, lobster, geoduck, fresh squid, dried squid, boneless duck feet, fatty beef, pig's kidney, goose chitterling, watercress, *udon* (thick wheat flour) noodles and shrimp dumplings. It's a communal way of eating that improves as you increase the number of people at the table. Lobster and other seafood come right from big tanks and are sweet, fresh and gleaming. Lobster is removed from the tail, minced and returned to the shell. Rock cod flesh is thinly sliced and laid over the body of the fish. Raw beef slices are fanned out *carpaccio*-style. The meal turns into a happy mess, as you use chopsticks to fish for lost bits of food while sauce dribbles about and platters are passed around and around. Nothing is spicy, but the kitchen will, if asked, provide a fine chili sauce. Plump whole scallops, writhing live prawns are a highlight. Service is informed and prompt. Decor will be familiar to anyone who frequents the newer Hong Kong-influenced restaurants in town. *$60. Licensed.*

Moutai Mandarin
1710 Davie St. 681-2288

Here is a very snazzy Chinese restaurant at English Bay, full of unexpected colors and textures. Despite the name, most of the best things on the menu are Szechuan: the famous dry-fried green beans; *hui kuo jou* (twice-cooked pork); shredded chicken Szechuan-style; shredded pork in chili, sour and garlic sauce. The shredded chicken is wonderful—deliciously moist cold chicken set atop pickled vegetables and ladled with a peanut sauce and roasted chilies. Moutai Mandarin chicken is also good, the meat in a ginger-rich glaze foiled with crisp, fried seaweed. *$25. Licensed.*

Park Lock
544 Main St. 688-1581

For Chinatown dim sum, this is a favorite; smaller than many dim sum houses, upstairs, with decor that has a fifties flavor and a kitchen that emphasizes seafood. It's tough to get in for dim sum, and reservations seem to be regarded by the restaurant as more fanciful than real: expect a wait. The food is prepared with minimum grease and delivers maximum flavor.

Among the favorites: big lumps of sweet scallops and shrimp forcemeat wrapped in a cabbage leaf and steamed; dumplings with ground pork, peanuts and cilantro; sticky rice with chicken and sausage; egg-noodle balls stuffed with shrimp; and—a textural oxymoron, like Japanese tempura in soup—pieces of Chinese donuts wrapped with soft rice noodles, sprinkled with sesame seeds and drenched in soy. *$18* (dim sum). *Licensed.*

Pink Pearl
1132 E. Hastings St. 253-4316

This enormous restaurant, renovated in 1990, produces remarkably good Cantonese food from a roaring-busy kitchen. Do not come here for quiet or coddling. Brigades of suited waiters survey the acreage and do a creditable job of feeding the masses. The predictable dishes are done well, but consider the deboned duck stuffed with a pasty taro root mixture, the whole thing fried and lightly tasting of five-spices powder. Big pillows of soft bean curd come stuffed with shrimp balls in a gingery brown sauce with shredded ham and mushrooms. The crispy "fried milk" (like fried blancmange, tasting slightly coconutty) comes with large, perfect prawns. Dim sum is also very good. Expect to wait for a table. *$30. Licensed.*

European

Chartwell

791 W. Georgia St., in the Four Seasons Hotel.
844-6715.

Woody, serene, Chartwell in the Four Seasons is one of the best restaurants in the city for either a power lunch or a long dinner in front of the fireplace with a good friend.

Under executive chef Wolfgang von Wieser, the flagship restaurant has been steadily getting better after faltering a bit when he took over from Kerry Sear a few years back. You'll find both lighter, original concoctions and bigger, more classical flavors, such as roast salmon with a full-bodied butter sauce tinged with maple and served with crisp celeriac chips or smooth, thin, smoked veal with bitter greens (dandelion, beet) and almost caramelized apricots that balance beautifully. And such stalwarts as wiener schnitzel with roast potatoes are great from a rare chef who actually knows how to make a proper wiener schnitzel.

With chef Ian Cowley, von Wieser changes the menu seasonally and supplements it with a modest fresh wine sheet. Over the years, menus have included grilled venison with hunter's ragout and *cepe spaetzle* (tiny mushroom-scented dumplings); chardonnay steamed Nova Scotia lobster, barely done, beautifully tender, served on fennel compote with shallot butter; grilled crystal squid with saffron risotto; strips of blackened pheasant on a citrus-yoghurt sauce with marinated beans; raw brussels sprout leaves with poached salmon and a remarkably delicate vinaigrette of pistachio and hazelnut oils;

and medallions of rare beef under a layer of boiled potatoes and a cap of Stilton cheese and beef marrow. The European approach is, appropriately for the city and the Four Seasons, complemented by Asian flavors and a selection of low-calorie options.

Service under the eye of maitre d' Angelo Ceccioni moves easily from crisp and competent by day to very fine at night: from the first appetite-whetting tidbits, through the wine service and on to old ports, you hardly notice how much money you are spending (entrées race beyond the $25 mark). *$90. Licensed.*

Adega
1022 Main St. 685-7818

The atmospheric rear room is loaded with stonework, rustic fixtures, rugged-fisherman murals and an old wine barrel. It's a perfect backdrop for the evocative, rich, solid Portuguese country cooking that features fish, meat and potatoes in unusual, but deeply flavored combinations. It's humble fare, but the food here can be delicious. For a meal that transports you to the Algarve, open with big, charbroiled sardines, then try the *bacalhau a gomes sa*, a succulent casserole made from potatoes, onions and olive oil, and of course the famous dried salt cod. Sublimely satisfying. Beef liver can be a tad overdone but nevertheless comes with savory, winey juices and potatoes. The pork with clams, another classic dish from Portugal, is consistently good. A real feast does not stretch the wallet. *$35. Licensed.*

Chesa
1734 Marine Dr., West Vancouver. 922-2411

Long a fixture on the North Shore for its straightforward, if slightly dated, continental fare that puts careful preparation and attractive presentation over experimentation. This is an intimate room where you can expect to see veal in cream sauce, kidneys Bordelaise, Italian and more northern European style noodles, lamb Provençale. Chicken and seafood dominate the menu, the latter treated with a gentle hand. Side vegetables are perfect—a good indication that the chef cares about all food. The absurdly delicious duck liver parfait, smooth as butter, made with port and amaretto and served with home-made toasts, is alone worth the trip. Good service, but needs better wine list. *$60. Licensed.*

CinCin
1154 Robson St. 688-7338

CinCin is a lovely room finished in comforting warm tones: terra cotta and dun-colored walls. Yellow lighting makes the place look like it's in perpetual sunset somewhere in the southern Mediterranean. But there is a lively mural of a whirling muse on the east wall, a big painting of some Bacchanalian revelry, and always a large crowd of happy diners to make this a busy room filled with enthusiasm. The menu is modest, but not small. It's a good take on Mediterranean ingredients—eggplant, peppers, beans, lamb, garlic. And it's a good take on rustic cooking methods—grilling, wood-fire cooking. The antipasti for one is generous and features grilled eggplant, marinated squid, green and black olives, and cold ratatouille. Prawns come with a wedge of grilled polenta and are dressed with a tasty lemon sauce—good for wiping up any of the olive oil/balsamic vinegar served with the bread. Chunky lamb chops are deliciously charred, with a good outdoor taste rarely found in most places advertising grilled food. You wouldn't call the service attentive, but you are never left waiting either. And you get plenty of smiles. *$70. Licensed.*

Santos Tapas
1191 Commercial Dr. 253-0444

This is a congenial, warm, neighborly place in one of the city's great neighbourhoods. On the small menu: traditional kale soup; garlic potatoes; small charred squid; grilled sardines the size of small perch; pork sausage; superb chicken livers. In short, beer-and-conversation food: good-sized portions, bite-sized prices. Salads and vegetables are less of a draw. *$25. Licensed.*

Vassilis
2884 W. Broadway. 733-3231

Vassilis is a family-run place with a solid core of regulars. The food is homey (prepared by the mother of the clan) and authentic and captures the coarse, simple, strong tastes of Greek cuisine. Oh, and what they manage from a small repertoire of olives, lamb, chicken, oregano, lemon, garlic, cheese, yoghurt, and the few vegetables that grow on the hard land of Greece. Roast lamb, meltingly rich, literally falls from the bone. Roast chicken, scented with lemon and oregano, is its equal and is a draw for repeat customers. Most entrées make quite a heavy meal, but you can always select five or six appetizers to make a lighter evening. Try the crunchy-crusted *keftedes* (Greek meatballs), excellent green and black olives, fine *skordalia* (potatoes and garlic puree) and *tzatziki* (cucumber, yoghurt, garlic dip) and *kefalotiri* (fried cheese). The calamari, lightly dusted with seasoned flour and quickly deep-fried to tenderness, may be the best in town. This is benchmark Greek cooking in Vancouver. *$35. Licensed.*

William Tell
765 Beatty St. 688-3504

Erwin Doebeli is the universally respected dean of the fine-dining scene in Vancouver. Consummate old-school European restaurateur and gentleman, he celebrated a quarter-century in business late last year. His restaurant bounced back from transition troubles after moving. Under chef Lars Jorgensen, it was steady and sometimes inspired; then Jorgensen took a job on Saltspring Island, and long-time French institution Pierre Dubrulle stepped in. A meal in early summer showed that the menu had swung back to cooking that is very traditional. A green bean salad with roast quail was very good (with a light hazelnut oil and chive dressing), and cherries jubilee was a wonderful, boozy soup of home-prepared cherries and ice cream. Service in this elaborately elegant, Old World room is impeccable, and you can expect good wine advice from Mark Davidson, one of the city's best sommeliers. *$80. Licensed.*

French

Cafe de Paris
751 Denman St. 687-1418

Streetside location, dark wood, red leather, gray marble tables, and just a wee bit eccentric (read overbearing) service make for an authentic bistro air. The non-voguish food at the heart of this place—sautéed calf's liver, kidneys with mustard sauce, pepper steak, herring and potato salad, omelets—is solid and satisfying, though perhaps showing a bit of fatigue. Rabbit pâté is chewy, not dry, grainy rather than coarse, and very mild; it's served with a delectable mouthful of creamy dill-cucumber salad. The tender liver goes head to head with Le Crocodile's for the best in town. Justifiably famous *frites*—lavished with a rich, very peppery pepper/brandy/cream sauce—equal glorious chips and gravy. There is a basic wine list with a few surprises in the cellar. *$45. Licensed.*

Le Coq D'Or
3205 W. Broadway. 733-0035

Interesting that the man who opened and sold Zeppo's—a successful restaurant of the New Italian persuasion—should decide to buck the trend and follow up with a bistro that makes an honest stab at raising the French flag in Kitsilano.

The room is lovely. The street-corner location means there are tall windows along two sides, bringing light into a warm space that has sunny, mustard-colored walls, white ceiling and trim, light-hued hardwood floor, dark wood cabinetry, a few judicious splashes of color from art and flowers—and that's it. Such a room gives those at work in the kitchen an advantage, because customers lean toward contentment even before they glance at the menu.

The menu leads with such appetizers as cognac pâté with roasted hazelnuts and steak tartare. Soups included onion and vichyssoise. Entrées run to *poulet roti coq au vinaigre* and pork chop with Dijon sauce and *frites.* These things were done right: the chewy, peppery, not at all pasty pâté; a thick slice of eggplant terrine with creamy goat cheese (the natural sweet succulence of the eggplant was perfectly answered by the sharp taste of the chèvre); and an *assiette charcuterie* of thinly sliced smoked lamb (which was a bit under-smoked), dry, rich game salami, spicy sausage, mustard aioli (garlic mayonnaise) and toast rounds.

Two entrées were equally tasty—first, a grilled pork chop on a creamy mustard sauce that was dotted with fresh corn and absolutely wailed with garlic; second, a slow-roasted lamb shank with red-pepper relish—meaty, pleasantly muttony, and falling off the bone. Kudos, too, for a simple plate of grilled scallops on an exceptionally lemony and light cream sauce. For dessert, the thick, rich curds of the crème brûlée, topped with sugar so carbonized it held whiffs of warm winter fireplaces. Solid intentions, here, and honest food.

As to breakfast—Le Coq D'Or addresses all the daily meals—this is an ideal room for café au lait, croissants with raspberry jam and orange marmalade, french toast with fresh berries, baked apple pancakes and asparagus omelets. The coffee and croissants were good.

The mid-sized wine list contains small vertical selections of bordeaux, including Pichon Baron and Pichon Lalande. The La Lagune, at *$31.95,* is an off-vintage bargain. Jazz piano was a pleasant addition. *$45. Licensed.*

Le Crocodile
909 Burrard St. (enter off Smithe St.). 669-4298

The great strength here has been the way chef Michel Jacob consistently turns out fabulous French food in the bistro mold—so fabulous that the reputation of the place now extends well beyond the city limits. It's not unusual to recommend Le Crocodile to visitors from Toronto or New York, only to find they've heard of it or have even been there already. Consequently, it's imperative to make reservations. The floor staff, who carry themselves with a mix of hauteur and humor, will try to fit you in without one, but when they say sorry, they're booked, they mean it.

Le Crocodile is what we think of when we muse about the ideal French restaurant. It's warm, urbane, not too expensive, and thoroughly delicious. Jacob shows brilliance with his light but still rich and flavorful sauces—they are intense and tightly focused—and his superb handling of fish (Dover sole) and meat (venison). He also achieves success with foods not often encountered on the average menu anymore: veal kidneys, calf's liver and plaice, a plain fish often battered and deep-fried in fish-and-chip joints.

Some favorites: grilled venison with port sauce and morels; earthy-tasting green beans; a salad with smoked goose and seasoned with the wild, herbaceous note of thyme; pasta stuffed with gamey buffalo on a tomato/cream sauce; a tart filled with orange cream and topped with fresh raspberries and the crème brûlée. Cheese omelets are done properly. Lunch time perfection: juicy pink calf's liver with herb butter melting over the top. Prices are more than fair.

Le Crocodile has become a fief, with Jacob its sire and the restaurant his castle. He sits high above not only the rest of the French restaurants in town, but most restaurants in town. *$55. Licensed.*

Chez Thierry
1674 Robson St. 688-0919

A mainstream French establishment serving escargots, mussels Americaine (in a lobster sauce with Pernod), perfect pepper steak, a six-chop rack of lamb with Dijon and rosemary sauce, and salmon bisque. The preparation is solid, although the food tends to come out a tad salty. The great strength of this forty-five seater is the service. Loyal patrons come for the familial care offered by rambunctious host Thierry Damilano, who on one occasion left the restaurant and drove to his home to get a pillow for a pregnant woman who found the seating uncomfortable. *$65. Licensed.*

La Toque Blanche
4368 Marine Dr., West Vancouver. 926-1006

A small restaurant with a West Coast cedar-and-green feel, relaxing thanks to lattice screens that keep the tables intimate but not claustrophobic. Snails wrapped in tiny filo triangles were shot full of garlic—one of the best renditions of escargots in town. Scallops in cream with chives were tender, if ordinary. There's an interesting strip loin with hazelnut, walnut and bourbon sauce. Duck breast in a pretty amber calvados sauce was served with crispy curlicues of crackling strewn atop—a nice way to treat this fatty cut. Desserts are traditional and good—strawberries and raspberries Romanoff, chocolate mousse, lemon tart. The plain but balanced wine list is exceptionally well priced. *$60. Licensed.*

Le Gavroche
1616 Alberni St. 685-3924

Certain French dishes achieve magnificence just in the description: veal sweetbreads with crayfish butter sauce and truffles; fresh shelled lobster with a sauterne-butter sauce; *profiteroles* (small puff pastry balls) with warm chocolate sauce. There is no confusion about what the chef proposes to do: he plans to build a classically proportioned dish using traditional techniques.

The dishes listed above are from the dinner menu at Le Gavroche, where fidelity to haute ideals remains the aim after thirteen years. This serious attitude fits with the place itself: a richly wallpapered upstairs room in a heritage house, containing several dining nooks, a fireplace, and an atmosphere that whets the appetite.

The pâté here was a good, coarse, meaty and peppery chew, exactly what you want, with a golden plum sauce not too sweet. Another winning appetizer: warm smoked quail with ginger/hazelnut vinaigrette; the split bird, arrayed on oiled greens, was delectable—smoky, succulent meat on those fighting little bones, a perfect small struggle before the entrée. And the entrée: pheasant breast stuffed with a celeriac forcemeat on a pool of wine-infused *demi-glace*. Six beach oysters poached in apple cider sauce made another main course, very fresh and very oystery, oozing black-green essences into the cream-finished sauce.

The upstairs room in this old house is charming, romantic, cozy—much like the dining rooms in small French hotels. The menu is more bistro-ish at lunch—lamb chops with a garlic and red wine sauce, beef filet with a Roquefort sauce; seafood salad with a lemon vinaigrette. The latter was good: lots of seafood, gently done, including sweet scallops and bits of salmon on a profusion of greens with a tart creamy dressing. So was a dish of fresh ravioli (stuffed with lobster and truffles) in a champagne cream sauce with salmon eggs.

This is no perfect restaurant, but when it is good it is very good. *$75. Licensed.*

Le Club
845 Burrard St., Vancouver. 682-5511

The Meridien Hotel fumbled when it closed Gerard and reopened it as Le Club. But now, with restaurant chef Olivier Chaleil taking firmer control, the place has re-established itself. Expect upscale renditions of humble French food: arugula sauce, pan-fried goat cheese salad, duck leg confit with white beans. And expect it to be exceedingly well-prepared. Chaleil has a love for strong flavors, especially garlic. The confit and beans have a powerful hit of the reeking rose and rosemary. Scallion dressing on the goat cheese salad is a super-concentrate that highlights the goat cheese and *mesclun* (mixed greens). Good advice here is to try anything with a sauce: in 1991 Chaleil was chosen as the best saucier in the city for intensely concentrated, yet surprisingly restrained creations. He's still on top. *$80. Licensed.*

Hamburgers

Milestones
2966 W. 4th Ave. 734-8616
4420 Lougheed Hwy., Burnaby. 291-7393
1210 Denman St. 662-3431

There are several Milestones restaurants now, but the original one at the Denman location, with its pseudo-Florida feel, is still the funkiest. There is a full menu, but the basic burger, juicy with a genuine smoky, charbroiled flavor, is the main attraction. Most burger joints do odd toppings—serving teriyaki burgers, mozza burgers, fried egg burgers, even blue cheese burgers—but here they are inspired. And delicious. Beef, whether whole filet or ground, lends itself to rich treatments, and the Milestones burgers get dressed with mango chutney and cream cheese, or pesto and cream cheese, or crab and béarnaise. A pepper-steak version, with creamy green peppercorn sauce and sun-dried tomatoes, is especially tasty. The curlicue fries, alas, are barely ordinary (and a side order is absurdly large). Lineups at the Denman location are the norm. *$15. Licensed.*

Hamburger Mary's
1202 Davie St. 687-1293

This is a neighborhood landmark made famous by its burgers, and infamous, perhaps, by the gay clientele it caters to. The burgers come as close as you can get to backyard-barbecue taste. The basic one contains a six-ounce patty grilled with the house's barbecue sauce, which adds just enough zip to keep the sandwich from tasting plain. The blue-cheese burger is juicy and thickly slathered in blue—a classic combination that surprisingly hasn't shown up in more places; the ranchero has fried egg and bacon for the seriously hungry. Fries glisten with fresh, clean oil and are outstanding—golden crisp, thick, fluffy. *$15. Licensed.*

Red Robin

200-752 Thurlow St. 662-8288
3204 W. Broadway, 732-4797
801 Marine Dr., North Vancouver. 984-4464
9628 Cameron St., Burnaby. 421-7266
112-4640 Kingsway, Burnaby. 439-7696
3000 Lougheed Hwy., Coquitlam. 941-8650

Red Robin is another chain of have-a-swell-time burger joints. There are other foods in the barbecue vein, as in the popular *fajitas*, but burgers are the draw. If you can get by the cutesy names on the menu ("Shrooms Kinda Mushroom Burger"), you will be looking at a great patty. The Whiskey River burger, slathered with onions, is rich (addicting?) and comes with a huge bowl of extra barbecue sauce. Highly recommended. *$15. Licensed.*

*Indian/African/
Lebanese*

Ashiana
1440 Kingsway St. 874-5060

Over the years this has been one of the city's better Indian restaurants. In mid-1992 it moved, leaving the rather tatty digs on Victoria Street for a spiffy, new, much bigger place on Kingsway and taking its *dil-kashe* cuisine (literally, food that makes you happy) with it. The tandoori-cooked meats are served sizzling on black iron platters—the Peshawari lamb *tikka* is especially good, meltingly tender and fragrant with spice. As required of any Indian restaurant worth its chapatis, the breads here are first-rate. Smoky stuffed *naan* (flatbread) and absolutely greaseless *pappadam* (crispy fried bread) are good companions to the luscious northern-style curries. *Shahi paneer* delivers home-made cheese cooked with peas, ginger, tomato, nuts and spice that is not, as in many restaurants, hard latex. *$30. Licensed.*

Natraj
5656 Fraser St. 327-6141

The menu is modest, and the decor, but for a few attractive paintings in the style of Moghul miniatures, is nondescript. But there is nothing modest about Indian cooking, and the fresh, home-kitchen flavors here do justice to the subcontinent's culinary glory.

Out of the tandoor comes a special *naan*, stuffed with a thick layer of chicken, almonds, currants and spice, redolent of the light charring effects of the hot oven: instantly one of the finest breads in town. Eggplant is fire-blackened—simply the best way to reduce eggplant to a smoky succulence—then mashed with herbs and sautéed with onion. The tandoori mixed grill is a platter of sikh kebab, extraordinarily tender chicken, mutton chunks and fresh onion and tomato, all sizzling on the hot black iron. *Malai kofta*, by contrast, is a study in soft textures—chopped fresh cheese, vegetables and mashed potato are fried as patties, then served under a buttery curry.

Seafood is a weak point, best avoided. Bombay fish curry was over-salted; prawns *jalfrazie*—marinated, spiced and sautéed with tomato, onion and sweet peppers—were hopelessly overcooked. Lots else is good, though. Milky Indian tea or beer go well from the *parathas* (flatbreads) to the final soppings of *dal* (lentils). For dessert, the mango ice cream is creamy and mango-aromatic, and the *ras malai*—curds in cardamom cream—is also good. *$30. Licensed.*

Rubina Tandoori

1962 Kingsway St. 874-3621

Like many small ethnic restaurants, the restaurant is longer on food than on decor. The main dining room suggests a mock Tudor dining barracks decorated with Indian art: swarthy princes conquering modest princesses on black velvet.

But you go for the food. You enter through a takeout lobby about as attractive as the street, but you know right away that greatness awaits: pungent, mouth-watering smells from cardamom, clove, garlic, and the very distinct mustard oil fill the room, and on the counter is an enormous container of lentils, nuts and spices in a superior Indian version of GORP (good ol' raisins and peanuts).

Try the *wadas* to start. These are small pancakes of crushed lentils, onions and spices, which go well with the excellent relishes and chutneys and pickles that carry on throughout the meal. The coconut and mint chutneys are at once cool and spicy.

The difference between the classic regional dishes of India comes through clearly here: chicken *makhani* (a butter curry) is delicious; chicken *bhoona jost* (dry northern-style curry) is rich with striking notes of anise and clove; lamb *vindaloo* (Groan curry) is smooth, tart, and swirling with a complex blend of cinnamon, clove, garlic, tamarind and black mustard seed. Breads keep to the generally high standard of Indian restaurants in Vancouver. The *naan* is good. The greaseless *pappadam* are flecked with biting black pepper.

Desserts keep to the Indian penchant for extraordinary sweetness but are very good. The *gualb jamin*—two milk-batter, deep-fried donut holes in rose-water-flavored syrup—can feed two. *$45. Licensed.*

Dar Lebanon

818 Howe St. 683-7927
809 Seymour St. 682-7000
1050 W. Pender St. 669-0500
2972 W. Broadway. 739-0608

As this chain has expanded, the food has kept fresh, spicy and not too salty or greasy. A quick look in the window at noon and you see these places filled to capacity with hungry lunchers (who must be careful about taking the heavy doses of garlic here back to the office). On several tries, the falafel in pita—a delicious, quick lunch—has been outstanding. Ditto the appetizers: marinated carrots, *tabouleh* (the bulgur, green onion, and parsley salad brightened with the taste of fresh mint), *babaganoosh* (eggplant purée given a hypergarlicky shot), and *hummus* (chickpea purée). *Lunch: $12. Licensed.*

Elissar
1961 W. 4th Ave. 736-9750

No straight-from-the-warming-tray lunch here; order the Elissar Delight, a pungent Lebanese stir-fry of chicken and coarsely chopped vegetables, and the flames will roar in the open kitchen. *Kafta kebab,* minced meat on skewers, served with tomato-sauced carrots, a spicy relish and rice, is a tasty, hypergarlicky dish. The chicken in pita, called *taouk,* is good too. Not that you should pass over what does come from the food bar: expect the traditional Middle Eastern side dishes to be well-executed. Try the *babaganoosh* (eggplant purée) with its sharp garlic bite. *$30. Licensed.*

Nyala
2930 W. 4th Ave. 731-7899

This is the city's most popular Ethiopian restaurant. It serves vigorous African cooking (with sirocco blasts of Indian and Arabian) that matches the heat of its sub-Saharan origins. Using bits of *injera* (crêpe-

and-crumpet-like bread), which functions as cutlery, scoop from a communal platter featuring fiercely hot goat stew, *fitfo* or raw, minced, cardamom-scented, butter-touched steak, chick-pea purée, assorted salads and side dishes. It's a convivial way to spend an evening—a chilly, rainy evening. *$25. Licensed.*

Raga
1177 W. Broadway. 733-1127
2120 Main St. 877-1661

Raga serves standard Indian fare, well-executed, but the fabulous breads baked in a tandoor oven nearly eclipse the rest of the menu here; breads like *paratha,* and *kulcha,* stuffed with onions and dried mango, make a meal on their own. Curries are rich and complex, and the lamb *vindaloo* is especially hot, vinegary—just right. The combination platters make a good choice on a first visit. *$40. Licensed.*

Italian

Il Barino
1116 Mainland St. 687-1116

Il Barino's understated storefront strikes a smart pose; inside, muddy-river tones mix with trompe l'oeil murals, a counter/display area of appetizing foods, and a roundup of overhead ductwork. Clichés now, but here they work, fooling you into thinking it's sunny outside and you're inside enjoying the cool shade. You can't exactly attribute quiet elegance to it, but neither would you want to show up in Ray Bans and espadrilles.

Il Barino was *Vancouver* magazine's Best Italian restaurant in 1992, maintaining—though only just, because Villa del Lupo is close behind it—a lead it quickly established after opening in December 1989. Not only has it so far survived a kitchen shake-up (chef Watoshi Ishakawa moved out; second chef Julio Gonzales left to open Villa del Lupo; in came the colorful Mark Potovsky), it seems to have become more focused in the process.

Like the decor, the menu sits somewhere between chic and rustic. Potovsky's two-pronged menu—dishes such as minestrone for the traditionalists, and such Italo-experiments as soft-shelled crab with fennel salsa for the foodies—is aimed at keeping Il Barino fresh in the apparently not-yet-saturated Italian market. The chef's signature salmon tartare is here. So are a tasty risotto with smoked chicken and medley of excellently prepared vegetables, and a down-to-earth dish of white beans, pepperoni, mascarpone and red pepper cream. Dessert: good home-made ice cream. *$65. Licensed.*

Il Giardino
1382 Hornby St. 669-2422

Critics have long ascribed the variability here to the presence or absence of Umberto himself, the don of the local Italian dining scene. Everyone agrees that the villa-like decor, from the courtyard to the lounge to the restaurant itself, is nonpareil. This is Umberto's flagship restaurant and still his place to be seen in.

Lunch brings the city's well-heeled crowd, who come to eat in one of the prettiest rooms in the city, and to linger and table hop. Not surprisingly, the noon-hour kitchen, perhaps appreciating the weight of the wallets in the dining room, seems more focused. This is the better meal to come for, although it would be hard to find fault with a long intimate evening, particularly while you sample from the impressive wine list. (Rumor has it that the most expensive bottle of wine ever sold in a restaurant was uncorked here.) Service is good, as you'd expect in a place run by the genial but particular Umberto. The staff can be unexpectedly honest, coaching you out of choosing a dish if they think it is not up to standard.

Grilled oyster mushrooms, tasting faintly of the sea, strongly of the grill and dribbled with a lemon dressing, are justifiably a favorite way to start. This is an example of the simple, rustic, satisfying food that is so popular now in other Italian restaurants—just remember, Umberto was doing this long before it became a trend. The classic tomato and mozzarella salad, lightly dressed, is excellent when the red fruits are in season; indifferent otherwise. *Carpaccio* is very good, the *bresaola*—a beefy version of prosciutto—

good if it hasn't been around too long, as it tends to dry out. Pan-fried lingcod with lemon-herb sauce was perfect, though the aioli (garlic mayonnaise) for rare and beautifully seared loin of lamb could have more garlic. It's not hard to drop *$50* for lunch. *Licensed.*

Villa Del Lupo
869 Hamilton St. 688-7436

One approaches Villa Del Lupo with the knowledge that it is run by people who had a hand in Il Barino, which did (or do) Italian better than anybody. Chef/co-owner Julio Gonzalez was the second chef at Il Barino; Vince Piccolo was general manager there and is manager/co-owner here. Mike Piccolo, Vince's brother, is sous-chef.

So, a meal begins well. The restaurant's focaccia bread may be the best in town, if you like it crunchy; the long thin wedges are flecked with herbs, redolent of olive oil and a nutty, roasted flavor. Try the wild mushroom mousse with a rose wine beurre blanc and prawn tails; Venetian bean and pasta soup; fettuccine with walnuts, garlic, thyme and extra virgin olive oil; pan-fried cod with tomatoes, lemon balm, chardonnay and olive oil; and half a free-range chicken roasted with herbs.

Meat dishes are bold and substantial. The *osso bucco* was a big mound that revealed a surprising delicacy, like seeing a linebacker perform an inspired pas de deux: the meat was lamb, not veal, braised with tomatoes, lemon, cinnamon and red wine, the sauce light and fragrant, the lamb throwing in a flavor of its own. It came with a good saffron rissotto. Roasted lamb loin with a black peppercorn and Cinzano sauce was also good—not as rare as ordered, but tender and rich with peppery roasted flavor. The sauce was a balanced reduction, and the meat came with grilled artichokes, grilled radicchio, sugar peas, asparagus and potatoes.

Faults? The service, while generous and attentive in all other matters, was obsessive regarding wine—a new dribble into the glass every two minutes until we were on edge, waiting, afraid to raise our glasses. And speaking of the wine: despite the staff's eagerness to serve, the list is too short and does not include vintages. *$60. Licensed.*

Bianco Nero
475 W. Georgia St. 682-6376

Bianco Nero is a gorgeous and stylish room, all black and white with tremendous splashes of color. This is the second of the Casadei family's restaurants (the other was Piccolo Mondo), and it is unmistakably a Casadei creation: the menu and weekly fresh sheet remain a challenge (so much sounds good), and the wine list is huge (the best Italian selection in town). The food runs from the traditional to the innovative. From one fresh sheet: julienned calf's liver with dry vermouth sauce and peas; sautéed prawns with cider-gorgonzola sauce; asparagus with nutmeg, butter and parmesan; and pasta with vanilla-lobster sauce. One outstanding meal: a delicious warm salad of venison liver with chanterelles in a rich brown sauce, served over greens; a house salad with grilled *bocconcini* (mozzarella cheese) and oyster mushrooms; grilled squid topped with thin slices of lemon, garlicky but light; and duck-stuffed ravioli on a wild-mushroom sauce. Service can be all over the map, from brusque to welcoming. This restaurant is a better bet for lunch than dinner. *$55. Licensed.*

Cafe Il Nido
780 Thurlow St. 685-6436

Owner Franc Felice has, if not completely revitalized Il Nido, at least given it some badly needed oomph. The menu changes several times a year and now does a good job of reflecting the seasons, if not exactly the dictates of the farmer's calendar: *cappelletti* (little pasta hats) filled with gorgonzola served with peas appear in cream sauce in winter; salmon with rhubarb, and halibut with avocado arrive in spring. First courses tend to be better than the mains, so try building a meal around the small dishes. Some samples: salad of mixed greens topped with tiny scallops bearing the black-brown signature of a quick sear; smoked chicken crêpes with fig chutney; a top-drawer dish of bow-tie pasta with an impeccable tomato sauce. An exception to this rule would be the pasta, which when ordered off the specials list is always satisfying. Standard wine list. *$55. Licensed.*

Napoli Restaurant
1660 Renfrew St. 255-6441

One of the city's best old-style Italian places—with kitschy decor. It would be lost in today's Italo-hip rage were it not for an above-average kitchen and an expansive, helpful host. Spaghetti *al amatriciana* was a fresh tasting tangle of tomatoes, onions, oil and smoky bacon, lacking only a good dose of musky *pecorino* (cheese). Fetuccine with black olives and anchovies was very good. There's more than pasta, however. After the usual veal dishes, such treats as a Sicilian dish of rolled veal with prosciutto and a sauce of eggplant, olives and brandy are favorites. The servings are huge: the pasta dishes can serve two people. Of the wines, the Salice Salentino is reliable and appropriate. *$50. Licensed.*

Piccolo Mondo
850 Thurlow St. 688-1633

The new management here appears to have picked up this old restaurant from the Casadei family (who own Bianco Nero) lock, stock and barrel. They've held on to the impressive wine list (with its broad and deep selection of Italian wines) but sensibly have chosen to warm up the service first before tackling the unmanageably long menu—especially the list of daily specials. The kitchen staff remains unchanged and continues to produce good food. As well as the usual Italian fare, there are some unusual savory dishes to be had: tripe in a mildly spicy tomato sauce;

silky smooth braised tongue with raisins and marsala wine at the end of your meal. They have a quaint habit of magically whisking the label off your bottle of wine and presenting it to you—emblazoned with the date—as a memento of your visit. *$65. Licensed.*

Saltimbocca
2201 W. 1st Ave. 738-0101

This is a sharp-looking, long and fairly narrow street-corner restaurant with windows running along two sides. What surprises and impresses is the open kitchen. It's a genuine working kitchen, not just a kitchen outpost for final assembly and shipping of dishes. There is plenty of entertainment here for the solo diner, and chef/owner Ken Bogas will ask you how you want your food cooked.

Saltimbocca continues the neo-Italian trend. The menu begins simply and plainly—antipasto *misto*, minestrone, spaghetti *carbonara,* scallopine with mushrooms, "classic" *cioppino* (seafood stew)—to satisfy the neo-traditionalists; the menu then sings a multicultural tune with an Italian accent: red chili linguine with crab, black beans and tomatoes; large scallops with papaya and cracked pepper; Chilean sea bass with lemon and extra virgin olive oil. Seafood, appropriate to both Bogas's background (he cooked at Umberto's Fish house, Barbara-Jo's, and the misfired Coyote Cafe) and a coastal city like ours, is emphasized. The wine list is friendly—a single page—and easily deciphered. It could use a few more Italian reds and more wine by the glass, but there are good wines to choose from: '88 Rosenblum and

Caymus Zinfandels, '89 Leonetti Merlot, '85 Frescobaldi Brunello, and Cloudy Bay Sauvignon Blanc. *$60. Licensed.*

Salute
1747 Marine Dr., West Vancouver. 922-6282

Salute can serve an excellent meal—a rustic plate of *fusilli* (spiral noodles) with potatoes, garlic, cabbage, and *pancetta* (Italian bacon) and a glass of ordinary red wine, for instance. The quality of the supper has much to do with the gracious, almost shy owner, Gamal Hanna, who runs the place without fuss, and with the plain white stucco walls, minimal showing of contemporary art, and quiet music—the perfect combination after an exhaustive day of work, traffic and crowds. The menu makes a nod to meat and seafood with about nine veal and shellfish dishes, but the bulk of the menu—twenty-two items—is pasta. A few sauces: scallops with pesto, vodka and cream, shrimp and peas, gorgonzola. Big chunks of soft bread and a spicy salsa-like antipasto accompany the meal. *$40. Licensed.*

Settebello
1131 Robson St. 681-7377

An Umberto joint, first of the upstairs Robson Street Italian restaurants, and it has managed to hold on with a menu centered on pastas and pizzas. The pizza is cooked in a wood-burning brick oven that produces the desirable blistering and supercrisp crust. Toppings are hip but not absurdist—smoked duck, *pancetta* (Italian bacon), artichokes and grilled radicchio, fresh tuna, capers, red onions, tomatoes, etc. The seafood pizza was remarkably good, tasting sweetly of seafood, and none of it was rubbery: squid, crab, shrimp, anchovies. The pie was not oppressively cheesed, either. And the pasta was good: spaghetti with fresh egg yolk, garlic and olive oil arrived crowned with a raw yolk; the whole dish turned creamy when the egg was stirred in. Cracked pepper and a bit of parmesan set it off perfectly. Convenient wine list here: all bottles are the same $18.95 price. The room, typical for the Umberto chain, is very pleasant, particularly the tiled and arbor-shaded big terrace. *$50. Licensed.*

Splendido
1145 Robson St. 685-2717

Even while puzzling about it, you have to admire the chutzpah of opening a big, upstairs Italian restaurant on Robson Street, when there's another big, upstairs Italian restaurant two doors down, another across the street, and a big, upstairs Mediterranean restaurant immediately opposite. This is the second Umberto restaurant in the bunch, and as usual it's a great room. Early menus offered a roasted tomato and chili soup, *gnocchi* (small dumplings) with *pecorino* (cheese), grilled beef on arugula, lamb with a salsa verde crust on marinated white beans, halibut with fava beans. There are some terrific appetizers: creamy crab cole slaw with threads of fennel and sweet pepper and a baking-powder biscuit flecked with sun-dried tomatoes; veal *carpaccio* (thinly sliced raw meat) with a creamy tuna dressing; a deep-fried *beignet* filled with creamy gorgonzola (more like a deep-fried folded crêpe); and a mixed-green salad with toasted pine nuts. A few appetizers and one of the passionfruit/champagne cocktails is enough for a good meal. Several microbrewery beers are available, and there are lots of wines by the glass. Downstairs there's a deli, serving *panini* (breads), salads, soups and desserts. *$50. Licensed.*

Umberto Al Porto
321 Water St. 683-8376

As usual, Umberto Menghi shows he is as good with interior design as he is with food. For a low-ceiling, basement room with no windows, this is a remarkably comfortable, authentic-feeling place. It's gorgeous, finished with terra cotta, glazed tile, big beams, and naked lights that give a rustic, but warm and convivial air for large parties (and there are enough nooks for couples). The many pastas—spaghetti with sausage, *pappardelle* (broad noodles) with rabbit and grappa-soaked grapes, fettuccine Alfredo—are stars. Also the meats—grilled chicken, steak with grappa and peppercorn sauce—are usually good too. There are two other reasons to go: the long Italian wine list with its astonishing run of chiantis; the Umberto Wine Club events which are held here and show the place at its finest. On one occasion: tender, rare lamb coated with a herby-anchovy mix and accompanied by perfectly cooked white beans with a hint of tomato and garlic. *$55. Licensed.*

Zefferelli's
1136 Robson St. 687-0655

One of the best-looking restaurants in town. Neat mix of Old World black and white prints, classical oils, abstracts, and oversize 3-D tropical fruits in a room of taupe stucco walls, oak flooring, and mahogany-colored furniture with dark green seats. There is an asymmetry here that keeps the room—and the diners—feeling fresh. The food is good, and, like the room, doesn't sacrifice comfort. Pick and choose from a well-executed antipasto menu of squid, properly grilled vegetables, chick peas and prosciutto, or take the sampler plate. Appetizers are generous; the delicious chicken livers pan-fried with sage and sherry on toasted bread, for instance, would make a fine light meal with a glass of crisp wine. The lunch menu includes some good munchies: *panini* sandwiches (Italian bread) and *crostini* (faced sandwiches). Pastas can be interesing (al dente noodles with a light and fresh tomato-and-basil margherita sauce). Chops are perfectly grilled. *$45. Licensed.*

Zeppo's Trattoria
1967 W. Broadway. 737-7444.

Service is up and down here, but the kitchen continues its good work with earthy, rustic foods. The menu changes frequently, making it difficult to predict what you will get, but certain flavors predominate: red pepper, crab, salmon, duck, capers, spinach, pine nuts. The hot antipasto plate included snails, duck sausage, shrimp in crispy filo, crunchy fried smelts, and a healthy dollop of aioli (garlic mayonnaise). Some dishes—the *conchiglie* (pasta shells) stuffed with Dungeness crab, for one—were mildly disappointing, but others were outstanding: tender grilled rabbit was fabulously gamey-tasting and came in a mouth-watering sauce sweetened with brown sugar and spiced with red chilies. There's a good selection of wines to match the rustic flavors of the food. The black chocolate pudding cake takes chocolate pâté-type desserts to new heights. *$60. Licensed.*

Japanese

Hoshi
203-645 Main St. 689-0877

When Tsutomu Hoshi opened this restaurant in Chinatown, Japanese businessmen found the place pronto. It went on to win the Best Japanese and Best Seafood in *Vancouver* magazine's 1991 awards and was a close second to Tojo's in both categories in 1992.

Hoshi shows an attention to detail, freshness, nuance, texture, originality and beauty in presentation—particularly with his sushi. He will put aside the usual offerings and serve up an astonishing array of exotica from the list of specials, twenty or so of the city's most interesting Japanese dishes, all reliably fresh and delicious and likely to startle. But you must insist here that you really want to try something unusual. It can sometimes be difficult making yourself understood. You must be firm. Then you might get something like steamed monkfish liver like a buttery seafood mousse in flavor, like foie gras in texture, served with grated radish and accented with a light vinegar. Or you may be served teensy whole squid, the size of your small finger, boiled and marinated in a sauce, that taste sweetly of the sea. Hoshi serves the best mackerel around—very subtle. And the smoky sauce on the *anago* (grilled eel) is less sweet than the usual. Prawn sashimi, candylike in its sticky-sweet deliciousness, can be preceded by deep-fried prawn heads, crunchy and fishy, which put a whole new spin on this dish. Geoduck is scored a zillion times and fabulously tender. And then when you do order the usual sushi and sashimi, everything has a freshness and perfection rarely encountered anywhere else in town. *$70. Licensed.*

Raku
4422 W. 10th Ave. 222-8188

Raku won *Vancouver* magazine's 1992 Critics' Choice Award for Restaurant of the Year. It's a globe-trotting tapas bar with a Zen heart, serving inspired food in haiku-like portions, run by a husband-and-wife team, transplanted respectively from Quebec and the Northwest Territories.

The room shows the degree to which Trevor Hooper and Laurie Robertson have been wooed by Japanese sensibilities. The shoe-box space is explicitly understated. White and gray are the dominant shades, and the few artworks—including Balinese pottery, modern Japanese woodblock prints and local bamboo art—are positioned with meditative deliberation.

The menu, a loose take on the preparations of Japan's *izakaya* (beer halls), works on theme and variation. On one side are the more or less conventional Japanese skewered *kushiayaki* dishes—the tiny teriyakis (chicken and onion; salmon), the barbecued and skewered meats and fishes, along with plain grilled rice balls, salad, and sashimi—everything in appetizer-sized portions. Then there are the variations on Indian, Middle Eastern, Southeast Asian, Caribbean, French or Italian cuisines—like lamb kebabs with hazelnut and date chutney, squid with saffron and red pepper mayo, and quail in muscat wine. Finally: bridging the conventional and the eclectic: *onigiri* (grilled rice balls) again, but this time made with artichoke-parmesan risotto; and grilled Japanese eggplant tinged with balsamic vinegar. This is a particularly finicky way for a chef to make a living—devoting all this attention to flavor and texture and touchy grill work, knowing that when dishes are so small a healthy eater can eat five or six. *$50.* Open for dinner only. *Licensed.*

Tojo's
202-777 W. Broadway. 872-8050

Tojo's and Hoshi run neck and neck, like thoroughbreds coming down to the wire. In 1992, Tojo's nosed out ahead to take the awards in *Vancouver* magazine for both Best Japanese and Best Seafood.

The photos of the celebrities and near-celebrities adorning the walls turn the restaurant into a bit of a shrine to Tojo's popularity with the non-Japanese, so the most straightforward advice is to belly up to the bar, make contact with the man in charge and announce your love of every creature that walks the earth and swims the sea. Then make a show of smacking your lips appreciatively at every offering (but that's not hard to do—the food is wonderful). There will follow a mix of specials and hot and cold dishes from the seasonal menu: it may be chrysanthemum-flower salad with sesame and flakes of dried bonito tuna; steamed pine mushroom; a dark wedge of bonito belly with minced radish, ginger and *ponzu* (lemon, lime and soy) sauce; a succulent, wee nugget of melt-in-your-mouth black cod. Of course, if you are stuck with where to begin, a bowl of Tojo's well-known buttery tuna, marinated with a wasabi-rich sauce of sesame, soy, and green onion is as good a place as any to begin. Oddly, service can be a bit cool and desultory if you are at the tables and not at the bar. *$70. Licensed.*

Aki

374 Powell St. 682-4032

This is one of Vancouver's oldest Japanese restaurants and though it may be showing its age a bit, it still has vitality. The decor is classic Nippon; you eat in paper-screen rooms sitting on tatami mats; the service is attentive and characterized by Asian graces; the food is the familiar Japanese menu—sushi, sashimi, deep-fried dishes, *udon* and *soba* (wheat flour and buckwheat flour noodles) in broth—but it is in no way pedestrian. *Chirashi sushi,* a simple style of sushi where toppings are strewn over a bowl of vinegared rice, is done with care here. Aki's version includes such treats as barbecued eel, sea urchin roe and fresh crab along with the usual tuna, salmon, squid, octopus, egg and flying fish roe scattered atop the rice Tokyo-style (in Osaka-style, the fish and rice are stirred up). The all-seafood tempura plate yields an assortment of prawns, crab, abalone, squid, salmon and scallops in a crisp, light, lacy batter. *$35. Licensed.*

Ezogiku Noodle Cafe
1684 Robson St. 687-7565

A dozen-seat, very mod noodle house with faux-stone walls, cobalt sconces and tiny hanging halogen lamps. You eat from stools at the noodle bar or by the window. The menu offers an assortment from curry rice to *gyoza* (fried dumplings). But the big bowls of noodles with pork, onions, sprouts and bamboo shoots are the reason you are here. The best is the *miso* version. This might not be the best place for Japanese noodles in town, but certainly is the grooviest place in which to eat them. And this makes a good spot for an impromptu meal while strolling the city's grooviest street. *$10. Licensed.*

Kitto
1212 Robson St. 662-3333

This is a vital and busy, busy, *busy* little Japanese grill. Crowds of late-night diners move through almost as fast as the cooks work the grill. Sit at the bar and order a selection of deep fried squid, soft-shell crab, and grilled eggplant sprinkled with flakes of *katsuo-bushi* (the strongly flavored dried bonito tuna). Barbecued squid is deliciously charred and not too chewy; prawn *gyoza* (fried dumplings) are a light change to the usual meat-filled version. The soups and tempura are excellent. Be sure to check the small blackboard near the door for specials and make sure you order a side dish of the hyper-crunchy pickles.

This is a good place for a substantial meal before the theater or a quick snack afterwards. *$25. Licensed.*

Koko
2053 E. Hastings St. 251-1328

This East Side sushi bar has the feel of a real neighborhood hangout; it's noisy, comfortable and a little shabby. It's also one of the city's best Japanese restaurants. The sushi and sashimi are always fresh and well-presented, and there are always a few surprises. Squid tempura and a cold ramen salad are favorites. Scallops mixed with flying-fish roe is a specialty. The *chirashi sushi* (done Tokyo-style with the toppings scattered on top of vinegared rice— Osaka-style mixes the fish and rice) was an extravagance of roes—sea urchin, flying fish, white fish, herring—along with the usual, meltingly fresh toppings. The bowl was topped with a quail egg cradled in a slice of red snapper. *$50. Licensed.*

Kyocha Ya
1536 Robson St. 682-1570

A welcome addition to the Japanese restaurant scene: bigger than a neighborhood sushi joint, but in that spirit. Prices are moderate; sushi and sashimi are well made, quick to arrive, impeccably fresh. River eel, tuna, quail egg, raw scallops, raw squid—all in the *nigiri* line are good, with generous pieces of fish. *Chirashi sushi* (toppings strewn over vinegared rice) is a lovely dinner for one. From the grill, try the squid, charred but tender. *Yaki onigiri* is a triangular block of sushi rice containing a plug of sour plum paste. The decor is bright: deep pink, navy blue trim, black chairs. The service, not always by people who speak much English, is warm and quick. *$35. Licensed.*

Noodle Express
747 Thurlow St. 669-1234

Here is a Tokyo noodle house in the heart of Vancouver, complete with goofy logo showing a cartoon chef in a little train. The noodles are very good— chewy but not floury or in any way underdone. The broth may seem a bit strong (deep brown, almost caramelized, oversalted) until you order the soy bean paste version, which is delicate yet full-bodied. There are several accompaniments to the basic bowl of noodles: barbecued (in fact, roasted) pork, bamboo shoots, pickled cabbage, spicy pickles, seaweed. The soy bean paste version comes with the roast pork, which is delicious, plus a boiled egg and vegetables. Absolutely essential is the sprinkling of fried garlic offered by the waitress. This is good, cheap eating. *$12. Licensed.*

Mexican

El Mariachi
735 Denman St. 683-4982

Even in Mexico, Mexican cuisine can be a muddy mix—the cilantro, chilies, masa, tomatillos and other herbs and spices swimming in too much lard, everything coming out merely filling rather than really enjoyable. But El Mariachi presents unusually clean-tasting Mexican food. The prawns with chilies, for example, are perfectly cooked, just past raw in the center and fiercely hot—the equal of any of the similar dishes presented in the city's Asian restaurants, which usually have the best grasp of seafood.

El Mariachi has the usual corn- and wheat-flour tortilla-based dishes—soft tacos, tostadas, burritos, enchiladas—but offers an unusual selection of salsas to accompany these and other dishes. For 75 cents each, there are sides of salsa *verde,* a warm, tart sauce of tomatillos, salsa *pasilla* (for fried food especially), searing salsa *serrana* (serrano chilis); it's fun to order several and conduct a salsa tasting while you wait for the main courses to arrive. *Filte al chipotle* (beef filet served with a generous puddle of creamy sauce made with the hot smoky chipotle chili) is incredibly tender; *quesadillas* (wheat-flour tortillas stuffed with cheese) have an inviting, grilled accent and are served with first-rate guacamole. *$30. Licensed.*

Cha Cha Cha
4490 Dunbar St. 737-7499

This little neighborhood restaurant serves some of the best Mexican food in a town that, by and large, has not been well-served by Mexican restaurants. Ingredients are not reduced to a meltdown of cheese, refried beans, sour cream, guacamole and salsa. Flavors are true and stand alone. Faults are minor and stand forgiven. The chicken *mole* is dark reddish-brown, sweet, rich, rounded, aromatic, with an undercurrent of astringent bitterness from the chocolate. The black-bean chili is served with charbroiled pork and delicious, slightly mealy, home-made tortillas; the pork can be overdone, though. Ditto with the meat in a "cubanette" sandwich with avocado, tomato, and black beans; good nonetheless. The chicken enchilada is one of the best, topped with a fresh and very "green-tasting" salsa *verde*. Cream of pumpkin soup is tasty. The menu lists thirteen tapas, so you can mix-and-match a dinner with friends. There are several wines by the glass. *$35. Licensed.*

Las Margaritas
745 Thurlow St. 669-5877
1999 W. 4th Ave. 734-7117

Two locations serve you big portions of saucy Mexican food on extremely hot plates. There is more "gringo" feel here than at some of the other Mexican eateries. Generally high standard in the kitchen, which uses peanut oil (not lard). It's easier on your heart, though some may feel that's not authentic. As usual in the city's Mexican eateries, heavily sauced items such as burritos, enchiladas, chili, fried foods. Excellent, fresh, hot salsa with all the flavors of onion, tomato, chili and cilantro coming through clearly. The bar serves first-rate margaritas to soothe your palate. *$30. Licensed.*

Pepitas
1170 Robson St. 669-4736
2041 W. 4th Ave. 732-8884
180 W. Esplanade, North Vancouver. 980-2405.

Joins with several other Mexican restaurants in serving plenty o' fun. Dinner is better than lunch. Good garlic prawns, *chorizo* (sausage), *seviche* (raw marinated fish), and *pisto con queso* (veggies and cheese). The *sopa de lima*—chicken soup with a shot of lime juice—is warm and refreshing on a rainy night. Choose heavily sauced items such as the enchiladas over the fried dishes. Guacamole is home-made and very good. The *paella* (seafood, rice and vegetables) can be excellent. Pepitas is best when it is busy. *$40. Licensed.*

North American

Bishop's
2183 W. 4th Ave. 738-2025

What clearly establishes John Bishop as one of the city's great restaurateurs is that his little whitewashed dining room presents better and better food, better and better service—every year. The worst that could ever be said about Bishop's is that it plateaued—temporarily—high above most other restaurants.

From time to time, Bishop toys with the idea of expanding his enterprise. He has just forty-eight seats arranged in a split-level dining room decorated with strong pieces of modern art, some of it from regular customers like Jack Shadbolt. But, this is his—and any successful restaurateur's—dilemma: if his place can't keep up with demand, should he add more seats, or is he so successful precisely because Bishop's is a perfect package, and any tinkering with it could spell ruin? Invariably, Bishop focuses his restless energy, polishing, improving steadily and surely.

Chef Adam Busby, in full stride now, shows dexterity with diverse victuals: a thick veal chop, blackened outside, rare and bloody inside, the whole slightly sweetened with marsala; fresh tasting, succulent snapper lightly coated with cornmeal, baked and served in a light chardonnay/curry sauce; pink calf's liver, dusted with cornmeal and served with rashers of homey bacon. Desserts are the comforting variety—blueberry cobbler, for instance.

Bishop's man on the floor, the gentle Sam Lalji, and the staff he directs are a shining refutation of the notion that Canadians can't provide good service.
$70. Licensed.

Joe Fortes
777 Thurlow St. 669-1940

The room—always great and spotlessly clean—has never been a problem here; the kitchen, which lagged behind the decor, seems at last to have found its stride, and now Fortes presents a good package for brisk, hip, uptown dining. The menu is cleverly designed: line drawings of seafood run down both sides, while the kitchen simply writes in a price next to what's available for the day. As in the American chophouses that this place evokes, portions are generous. Seafood is the focus, most of it pan-fried or grilled. Grilled scallops with a roasted corn sauce are tender and smoky, and this is one of the best places to get good fresh oysters. A sampler plate of tuna, marlin and cod with three salsas yields three pieces of tasty fish. This may be the only regular source of duck leg confit. The bar stocks a great selection of single malt whisky too. *$60. Licensed.*

Raintree
1630 Alberni St. 688-5570

This is a distinctly local place, and one has to say it has gone a long way to elevate and market the idea of a regional approach to food in Vancouver. The once comic zeal here for the regional concept is now a more mature enthusiasm; the scaled-down menu is seasonal and features dishes from West Coast seafood to B.C. fallow deer—with a heavy emphasis on organics and healthy cooking. Despite overwhelming public support—it consistently takes top spot in *Vancouver* magazine's Reader's Choice Awards—the Raintree has struggled. Chefs have changed three times; the current ones—and the first men in the kitchen—are Anthony Hodda (ex of CinCin), and sous-chef Robert Young (from the Santa Fe Cafe). Still, the effort seems to be paying off. They lead with some good concepts: a fixed-price lunch that's ready in ten minutes and a wine list that is a fine introduction to wines of B.C. and the west coast of the U.S. *$60. Licensed.*

Alma Street Cafe
2505 Alma St. 222-2244

Of the fine food and live music served here, the music may even be better. June Katz is now the hostess/chanteuse, and other local jazz talents—bassist Rene Worst, pianist Ron Johnson, tenor saxist Fraser MacPherson—often perform here. Like the music, the cafe's menu has its roots in street culture. The food appears to take inspiration from the sixties and seventies, when 4th Avenue was in its earthy oaty heyday. The kitchen has a penchant for seeds, nuts, berries and tofu—as in salad of greens, roasted nuts, radicchio and sprouted organic sunflower seeds, or salmon rolled in sunflower seeds and pan-fried, or loin of pork with blueberries, or filo pastry filled with vegetables and tofu. Earthy and substantial to be sure—a salad of greens, daikon radish and strawberries topped with miso dressing is a chunky meal—but this is far away from the old organo-macro-bio diets of twenty years ago. *$45. Licensed.*

Barbara-Jo's
2549 Cambie St. 874-4663

Barbara-Jo's is a small, personal restaurant in an unlikely location that has succeeded in part because so many loyalists know soft-spoken Barbara-Jo McIntosh from her catering days. Both the room and "elegant home cooking" are simple, direct and appealing. Lots of cream, dark green and black in the uncluttered decor. The menu is Southern-influenced: seafood stew with corn sticks, bourbon prawns, chicken and artichoke stew, oven-barbecued pork with sweet-potato fries. But it is possible to eat very lightly here: salade Niçoise, lemonade and fresh raspberries constitute a light lunch. Another, more substantial lunch includes Kentucky blue-corn crêpes with a creamy parmesan sauce, tomato, peppers, turkey and bacon. The crab cakes are some of the best in Vancouver, and prawns with a pear/mango chutney are grilled just right. The wine list is short, but everything is available by the glass. *$42. Licensed.*

Beach Side Cafe
1362 Marine Dr., West Vancouver. 925-1945

This canny little North Shore restaurant is a partnership of owner Janet McGuire (a Pan Pacific Hotel alumnus), chef Carol Chow (Bishop's, Settebello) and manager Ken Brooks (English Bay Cafe)—folks who have swum in the sharky waters of the Vancouver restaurant scene and survived.

Their food is a mixture of Californian, Tuscan and

Asian influences that might seem old hat. But dish after dish is straightforward and good, and that's an encouraging sign: grilled lamb sausages with rosemary, white beans and Dijon mustard; shrimp cakes with avocado and tomato salsa; Danish back ribs with orange-soya glaze; tomato, jalapeno and cilantro soup; stir-fried prawns in Thai curry; and pork tenderloin stuffed with pears and cinnamon with bourbon sauce.

Starters are a real strength. Grilled oysters with a thick, homemade lemon-chive mayonnaise proved absolutely delicious. One bite of those oysters and, for a few savory moments, everything else seemed incidental to the meaning of life; they were succulent, steely fresh and full of grill flavor. Mild blue cambozola cheese was given a thick coat of crushed hazelnuts, baked until soft, not gooey, and served with roasted garlic. Grilled beef filet was rare as ordered (if a bit chewy), and came with deliciously seared, nearly crisp oyster mushrooms, garlic mashed potatoes and a horseradish cream. Breast of chicken in tandoor spices was perfectly done and very juicy, although the spices tasted rather curry-powder-issue and seemed superficially worked into the meat. The chicken came on coconut basmati rice, which was pilau-dry and basmati-fragrant, but without any hint of coconut richness. A fruit chutney tasted of pineapple and clove.

Desserts pick up the pace again, at least on one side of the table. The crème brûlée is not dense and eggy, but has an almost billowy custard softness that contrasts with the thin splinters of the caramelized sugar. Service is impeccable from start through the wine and on to dessert.

Lunch is just as convincing—nothing fancy, but nothing less than good, either: a tart, citrus-tinged jalapeno/tomato soup that was warming, refreshing and not overconcentrated; an equally tasty warm chicken salad of bacon and chicken bits with zucchini and green onion on greens, all under a creamy dill dressing and a generous layer of freshly grated parmesan. The size of the serving is perfect—this is another finely tuned dish, balancing smoky bacon flavors against the cheese, the cream and the lettuce crunch. As warm chicken salads go, the best. Also good: a sandwich of grilled turkey breast on grilled bread with a mild sage mayo and cranberry chutney.

This restaurant shows promise and has what a cafe needs most: a convivial, neighborhood feel. *$52. Licensed.*

Delilah's
1906 Haro St. 687-3424

Delilah's presents high camp and good times in one of the city's most characterful restaurants. They do not take reservations, so everyone crowds around the bar that launched the martini fad in this city. The decor is plush, lighting low, the room small and the tables close together in an intimate room on a quiet, parkable West End street. The food can be very good: a pepper steak with mustard seed aioli (garlic mayonnaise) and potato cakes is superb. Ditto skewers of lamb, which arrived still sizzling from the grill. Accompanying vegetables are sometimes unusual, as in sweet potatoes and beets mixed. You fill out your own order on a slip of paper that later becomes your bill. At $24 for five courses, it's a steal. *$50. Licensed.*

Earl's
303 Marine Dr., North Vancouver. 984-4341
1185 Robson St. 669-0020
901 W. Broadway. 734-5995
4361 Kingsway, Burnaby. 432-7329
4335 Lougheed Hwy., Burnaby. 291-7380
10160 - 152nd St., Surrey. 584-0840
1601 W. Broadway. 736-5663

Of the fresh-food, forward-looking restaurant chains in town, Earl's remains the best. A large part of its success comes from its progressive policy of taking its staff around the world to shop for high-quality ingredients for its menus. Each location has its own theme, as created by restaurant designer David Vance, yet they all maintain a cheery, have-a-good-time atmosphere. Like the bright decor are the staff, who can sometimes be achingly chipper. On the other hand, they frequently show uncommon skill at handling young children, so these places make good bets for a family dinner. Earl's Cafe Fish (1601 W. Broadway) serves excellent blackened fish. The Earl's on Lougheed Highway does the same with a blackened-chicken Caesar salad. All serve decent hamburgers that go well with the Albino Rhino ale brewed for the chain by the Whistler Brewing Company. Also good with the ale are the crispy-dry ribs with coarse salt and cracked black pepper. Good value wine list and fresh fruit and non-alcoholic margaritas too. *$35. Licensed.*

English Bay Cafe
1795 Beach Ave. 669-2225

At its best, the main, upstairs restaurant can serve very good food. Sea scallops and Arctic char as delicious as anywhere on interesting balanced sauces (dill-dijon hollandaise, grapefruit beurre blanc) have appeared over the years. This is all laudable in a location that seems a license to print money—so good is the West End bay-facing location. There is nothing more gratifying than scoring a window table here. So popular is the view that this institution can pack in the crowds even late at night during record-breaking rains. Things can fall down a bit on the details—ordinary vegetables underdone, only adequate pastas and actually getting a table, even with a reservation, can mean a wait. The wine list, once quite advanced for the city, appears to have been scaled down, but there still are some surprises. Downstairs, the bistro offers an informal menu. *$70. Licensed.*

Five Sails
999 Canada Place, in the Pan Pacific Hotel. 662-8111

Given the rich but bland interior, ask for a window seat for a view of the Canada Place sails to the North Shore or toward Stanley Park. The menu manages to be both restrained and eclectic, from marinated venison medallions with rhubarb sauce to Mongolian glazed chicken with corn relish. The applewood smoked lobster chowder was delicious: light, coral pink, perfumed with smoke. The costly entrées showed that capable hands were at work in the kitchen, but sometimes lacked the all-round quality that completely satisfies. A seafood fantasia contained superb cinnamon-smoked salmon, although the rest of the plate paled by comparison. Desserts can be grand: try any poached fruit in puff pastry. Service comes from a slightly quirky multinational brigade, clockwork but not impersonal. *$80. Licensed.*

Harpo's
1215 Thurlow St. 685-8410

This is chef Patrice Suhner's fast-food joint, and some people will already know you get the same outstanding fries he makes at Cafe de Paris, too. The menu is essentially limited to barbecued chicken and fries, but this is not your typical barbecued chicken, you understand: instead of blackened fowl slathered with sweet, catsupy sauce, you get a juicy, rosemary-roasted bird with a caramel-colored, crispy skin. Make sure you order the pepper-cream sauce for dipping the fries and mopping up with bits of chicken. There are a few so-so salads to fill in the missing food groups. Seating is token so this remains a take-out establishment. *$10.*

Mescalero
1215 Bidwell St. 669-2399

It enjoys the West End's finest neighborhood location—a cream-colored, tile-roofed building just off Bidwell that in its current incarnation vaguely evokes the Alamo. It can quickly fill up with those seeking a serious taste of southwestern cuisine. The restaurant maintains considerable loyalty to the inventory of lime, pumpkin seeds, papaya, corn, tomatillos, cilantro, and, of course, chilies of all kinds, with dishes like grilled trout with papaya salsa; tuna, shark, and salmon *seviche*; New York steak with five hot peppers. The kitchen runs until 11:00 p.m., and the tapas bar stays open until midnight. *$70. Licensed.*

Mocha Cafe
1521 W. Broadway. 734-5274

This place has the inviting working-class feel of the little cafes of France, although it is in no way French. It started as a lunch spot but now includes dinner. Excellent muffins, perfect eggs Benedict and basic well-executed sandwiches—tuna, ham and cheese—plus three pastas, turkey burgers and pizza are served for the noon meal. At night, the pace slows, the lights dim, and it can be a pleasant thing to spend an evening in one of the cozy, old-style cafe booths. Dinner can be inventive—filo filled with water chestnuts, or shrimp with an Indonesian sauce. It is a good idea to call and see what will be on chef Don McDougall's mind; as late as 1:00 p.m. he may have yet to decide what he will do with, say, a fresh salmon that arrived at his back door that morning. *$45. Licensed.*

Monterey Lounge & Grill
1277 Robson St. 684-1277

As with many hotel dining rooms in this city, the place is suffering from low occupancy—which is a shame, because one of the city's more talented chefs, Anne Milne, presides over the kitchen. Californian/

American is the theme, accented with notes from Italy and the Orient. The emphasis is on seasonal produce—Milne even keeps a rooftop garden. Expect good advice on fresh oysters. There's the city's best blackened fish: charred and crusty outside, moist inside—not watery—and tasting of hand-selected spices, not some prepackaged Cajun mix, and the rest of her seafood follows suit. Brunch is straightforward eggs-and-whatever, but with one or two dishes like spicy sausages and polenta in mustard for zip. Expect good food even when Milne is not in the kitchen. *$50. Licensed.*

Sophie's Cosmic Cafe
2095 W. 4th Ave. 732-6810

An eclectic, junky, artsy (check out the Ken Lum photo art), vaguely retro neighborhood cafe that manages to be goofy and comfortable where so many others in town have fallen flat: by now it feels like a friendly, long-established neighborhood hangout. You're comfortable here. The food is usually good and sometimes *very* good: try Jimmy's Greek beef burger—a good, juicy patty with a creamy dill/feta cheese sauce on a fresh sesame-seed bun with red onion and veggies—with a thick, old-fashioned milkshake. Other offerings: Louisiana po' boy oyster sandwich, chicken burritos, blackened-chicken pasta. Omelets, french toast and Belgian waffles for breakfast. Small sidewalk patio. *$35. Licensed.*

Pizza

Flying Wedge
1937 Cornwall Ave. 732-8840
1175 Robson St. 681-1233

The laid-back staff can be a bit overwhelmed when crowds arrive, but a little patience is rewarded. Four "Wedge Classics" and one daily creation are usually available, though there can be problems keeping up with the demand. Good, light whole-wheat and herb crust, with a medium weight of cheese. One version contains shrimps, onion, zucchini and asiago cheese. The Tropical Pig has ham, pineapple and almonds. Your slice is reheated in the pizza oven when you order, so they have none of the problems associated with keeping pizza under heat lamps. *$2.75 per slice. $3 for the special. Whole pizzas, $11.50 to $23. Licensed.*

Lombardo's
120-1641 Commercial Dr. 251-2240

Think pizza, not location, when you head to Lombardo's. There are a lot of brick-oven joints in town, and you will find endless arguments about who makes the finest pizza. This is the best in town. It tastes like it came straight from Naples.

Watch Marcello Lombardo work big balls of soft dough into lumpy disks, with a curious motion that looks like he's hammering out the last chords of a Scarlatti concerto. He is the master of what is essentially a simple food, but one that many chefs have a difficult time making well. The wood-burning brick oven, flickering orange with hardwood charcoal, turns out a delicious, thin, blistered crust with a wheaty cracker-like flavor. A simple tomato sauce and an understanding hand with cheese lets the other toppings stand out. The tastes are scattered about the pizza in classic Italian fashion: one bite yields a marinated artichoke, the next tart capers, the next a powerful shock of anchovy. *Large pizza: $22.95. Licensed.*

Passionate Pizza
1387 W. 7th Ave. 733-4411

This little store is the pizzeria most serious about the California-born, Wolfgang Puck-style of pie. Here are some offerings: Puck's Pizza, with mozza, smoked bacon, red peppers, red onions, feta, asiago, eggplant; Provençal, with green olives, feta, eggplant and caramelized onions; Granville Island Gourmet, with gorgonzola, chunky roasted garlic, caramelized onions, toasted pine nuts and no tomato sauce. They carry Cinotto, the bitter-orange-flavored cola from Italy, which seems appropriate, and they will also deliver. *Large pizzas: $16.50 to $19.50. Licensed.*

Did's Pizza
630 Davie St. 681-7368
823 Granville St. 689-8866

Did's Pizza is a pair of street-style, rough-and-ready, pizza-by-the-slice joints; the Davie Street outlet is the better, very busy with hungry nightclub refugees crowding in around 2:00 a.m. The decor has been upgraded here from simple back-alley to a *Blade Runner* set with a CD-jukebox. When the place is busy, the pizza is good: a herby tomato sauce on an honest crust. They serve a rotating selection of pies, by the slice or whole, mostly to go, since seating is limited. The pesto pizza is particularly good and tastes of sweet fresh basil. It can be one of the best slices in town when fresh. The Sicilian is very peppery and tastes of *pancetta* (Italian bacon). When the place isn't busy, the crust becomes limp and the mozza hardens. Conclusion: go late. *$2.75 to $16.65. Licensed.*

Pizza Rico's
1106-1/2 Robson St. 669-2900

This is a tiny, no-frills, cluttered, by-the-slice pizzeria and Far Side gallery. The place is lined up out the door at lunch. For newcomers, the owner's brusque patter can be entertaining or intimidating, depending. (He has asked people using cellular phones to leave.) Three or four varieties of pizza are featured on the menu each day. The crust is superior, with a satisfying nutty flavor, but a heavy dose of cheese obscured the more subtle tastes on Rosie's Favorite: broccoli, tomato and feta cheese. The potato-and-garlic pizza is unusual and worth the visit. *$3.50 per slice.*

Slice of Gourmet
1152 Denman St. 689-1112

Another of the tiny, by-the-slice, sidewalk "gourmet" pizza places that have been popping up around town, serving pizza in the Pizza Rico's mold. The

Greek slice has eggplant, onions, feta cheese and oregano; the hummus pie has the chick-pea purée plus olives, onions and gouda cheese. There's pizza with roast lamb, even pizza with creamed broccoli and cheese. This is very heavily loaded pie—one slice is a meal, unless you're starved; the crust is good but can get soggy. Bright decor, and almost every seat is a window seat, with views of the Denman/English Bay action. Friendly family service. *About $3 per slice; large pizzas $15. Licensed.*

Seafood

The Cannery
2205 Commissioner Rd. 254-9606

The bar looks like something out of a Robinson Crusoe sitcom, but the view is impressive and the location—amid the packing plants and factories—feels good. The menu conservatively keeps up with the trends, if that's possible, and offers a large selection of fresh fish, ranging from sea bass to grouper to salmon. The food has generally been solid: simply grilled *tilapia* (mild white fish), a bit ragged from the grill but not overdone, on a competent cream-based sauce; nicely barbecued prawns that were not in mint condition to begin with; and a creditable bouillabaisse with tender seafood in a tomatoey broth that hinted of Pernod. The Cannery's long, prize-winning wine list will have just about anything you desire to match your fish. *$50. Licensed.*

The Amorous Oyster
3236 Oak St. 732-5916

As the name suggests, you get oysters here, from the familiar Rockefeller version to newer creations, like oysters with black bean sauce or green chili pesto. But there is good work with other seafood: clams in Pernod and orange were tender and not overwhelmed by the liquor; sole with julienned vegetables, wrapped in lettuce, was given an interesting note by the addition of *hoi sin* sauce. This is an informal but not casual dining room run by an all-female staff who score big points in the battle of the sexes with their thorough service. Wine list is heavy on American selections. Unusually observant staff brings an icy carafe of lemon-scented water before the diner has to ask. *$50. Licensed.*

Bud's Halibut and Chips
1007 Denman St. 683-0661

In an old-fashioned English joint such as this, you almost want the decor to be sliding towards dingy. Indeed, there is something suspicious about a tony fish-and-chip house. Here the room is a bit tatty but the halibut is top-notch. Each piece dressed in a slightly nutty-tasting amber-brown crust that is neither too thin nor too thick. The oysters here, also battered and deep-fried, are good, too. This is food perfectly matched by nut-brown ale, which it so happens they have on tap. *$18. Licensed.*

The Only Seafood Cafe
20 E. Hastings St. 681-6546

A great greasy spoon, a great diner. Out-of-towners wonder what the fuss is about, and those afraid of Hastings Street stay away, but regulars know that there is good fish to be had in Vancouver's oldest restaurant: fried oysters and skate, halibut and chips, sole almost blue if so ordered. The little booths are almost always full, but there are also counter stools. If you've never been, brave a visit just to experience the atmosphere. *$25. Licensed.*

Pajo's
Government Wharf, Steveston

With no phone and no street address, you find this small take-out place by heading to the end of characterful Moncton Street in Steveston and then following the signs to the government dock on the south arm of the Fraser River. It's the bright yellow hut floating—yes, floating—among the fish boats. It's hard to beat this place for ambience. And it's hard to beat the fish, too. Big, piping-hot pieces of halibut or cod in a crunchy batter. Fries served as they ought to be—in paper cones. Mushy peas are a popular side dish. Seating is rustic and outdoors only. *$14.*

Salmon House on the Hill
2229 Folkestone Way, West Vancouver. 926-3212

What they do well here they do very well: grill fresh seafood over smoking alder. For those who suppose the restaurant is riding on the coattails of its breathtaking view, the menu turns out to be far from conservative. Fresh sheets have included oven-caramelized salmon jerky on bannock bread, grilled marlin with a light sauce of passionfruit. The standing menu has more fish: deep-fried won ton stuffed with salmon, shrimp, green onion, Chinese black bean; escargots with Riesling, sun-dried tomatoes, grapes, and prosciutto. Although the kitchen seems to have difficulty getting the details and trimmings right for these dishes, few restaurants can match this place for grilled fish that is crispy outside, deliciously moist, and just past rare inside. *$60. Licensed.*

Southeast Asian

Sawasdee
4250 Main St. 876-4030
2145 Granville St. 737-8222

This is the original restaurant in a now ubiquitous cuisine, and the joviality here is welcome, especially compared to the suffocating seriousness sometimes encountered in other Asian spots. As for the food, it's still among the best Thai food in the city. This was the winner in *Vancouver* magazine's 1992 Best Asian category, and it didn't win because of elaborate cooking. This is homey and carefully done: *Om kah* (the distinguished soup of spicy chicken broth counterbalanced with coconut milk) is nowhere better done in this city; the fried vermicelli dish *mee grob* is more flavorful than the blander versions found elsewhere, too. Recent dinners have featured excellent flower-shaped dumplings stuffed with sweet minced chicken; prawns with just the right texture in fresh basil, green pepper and onion; and a coarse, fiery beef salad. The hustle of an (often) overcrowded weekend night suits the lively personalities of the staff, who are always accommodating. *$35. Licensed.*

Phnom Penh
244 E. Georgia St. 682-5777

Winner of *Vancouver* magazine's 1991 Best Asian category and still one of the best of its kind. The restaurant serves Cambodian, Vietnamese and Chinese dishes; a second location has appeared on W. Broadway—it's bigger and fancier but offers identical food. Nowhere is deep-frying done with a more delicate touch. Try the spicy garlic squid, deep-fried in a light batter and served with a dipping sauce of pure fresh lemon juice and black pepper. Or try the equally good spicy garlic prawns, which are butterflied and so perfectly lightly crunchy that the shells *must* be eaten. The marinated butter beef is a Southeast Asian *carpaccio:* slices of almost raw beef with crunchy browned garlic on a sweet, tart fish sauce. Exemplary hot and sour soup—the finest of its kind, neither too sweet nor too tart, fragrant with cilantro, green tomato and pineapple. Good pork chop dinner plates and salad rolls. The room is bright and snazzy, and there is always a large supply of attentive service staff. *$25. Licensed.*

Viet Nam Cuisine
410 E. Hastings St. 253-5530

The Vietnamese are especially good soup-makers, and one of the best bowls can be had here: *pho*—the standard beef broth/noodle/coriander soup served in Vietnamese restaurants and soup cafes all over town—is a straightforward belly-warmer; "rice noodle in soup" is a more complex oddity. The noodles are slippery, transparent strands like big, bean-thread noodles, cooked not al dente but to a unique and peculiar resilience. They resist chewing and slip down with a life of their own; it is an engaging experience. The broth has good body, and a whole jumble of tasty bits comes with it: fried pork rind, fried onion, slices of roast pork and a sprinkling of ground pork, a prawn or two, maybe a chunk of fake crab, some fresh bean sprouts, lime and green chilies.

The soups make a filling meal for under $5, but remember that this is a full-menu restaurant. Recommended: the salad rolls (four varieties), the chicken hot-pot and the brochettes. Iced coffee and fresh lemon soda are refreshing accompaniments. Expect zero decor. *$15 (soup, salad rolls, coffee for two). Licensed.*

Arirang House
2211 Cambie St. 879-0990

This is the best Korean U-cook in town, the food a fugue of the seven basic tastes in the repertoire—ginger, garlic, soya, green onion, black pepper, sesame oil and toasted sesame seed—played out in a robust fashion that one expects from a cold-climate country. Try rice with "mountain" vegetables for a comforting lunch; Korean-style beef tartare, boiled squid with hot sauce, and the "garlic lover's special," a roll-up of beef and huge chunks of garlic, round out a dinner. Chili and vinegar come to play in *kim chi* (pickled chinese cabbage). Beef plays a central part in the Korean diet and here on the menu. A group can spend a long evening fiddling with *bulgalbi* (marinated ribs) or *bulgogi* (marinated filet) on the table-top grill. Seafood, even tripe, augments this private barbecue, which is accompanied by a selection of pickles and condiments. Kitchen-prepared seafood can arrive overdone, and the service can be tentative or stubborn, but the news is generally very good. *$40. Licensed.*

Bangkok House
143 E. Broadway. 873-2221

The food here has a quality that suggests a Thai mom is at work. The exotic flavors of southeast Asia—hot chilies, tart lime juice, lime leaves, lemon grass and garlic—are here but come out rounder, less sharply distinguished, than other Thai restaurants, though it's still deliciously homey. The menu emphasizes seafood. *Tord mon* (fried spicy fish cakes) are crisp and naturally sweet, not too oily. *Dom yum goong* (Thai hot and sour soup with shrimp), accented with fresh coriander, is a rustic, full-bodied broth. They present an extraordinary lunch deal: *dom yum goong* and an entrée, perhaps *pat pick pla* (fried sole in spicy Thai sauce), or *paneng nua* (marinated beef with spicy sauce and fresh basil), or *kang kai* (chicken with coconut milk served with Thai spring rolls) or one of five others, for just $5. *$30. Licensed.*

Montri's
2611 W. 4th Ave. 738-9888

The floor-to-ceiling windows, distinctive pleated curtains and central display case set this Thai restaurant apart from many others. The food, too, is considerably above average and carefully prepared. One dish stood out: *gai-yang,* a superb example of Thai-style barbecued chicken, marinated in coconut and spices, then rigorously charbroiled. Other choices: a gingery fish curry, in which the fish was not overcooked; a curry of pork with green beans and Thai basil in coconut milk; and a green curry with red pepper, bamboo shoots and tiny eggplants. If you like your food hot, be sure to stress this with the staff, as they tend to pull back on the chilies. Service was charming, and the food came quickly. *$35. Licensed.*

Nonya Baba
1091 Davie St. 687-3398

Nonya-style food—a mixture of Chinese ingredients and Malay spices cooked in a way that perfectly mingles the two cultures—has made this humble place famous. Even if you haven't eaten from Singapore's hawker stalls, you'll appreciate such delicacies as *laksa* (coconut milk soup), chili prawns, and *rendang* (a delicious, dry curry flavored with cinnamon, cloves, ground coriander, cumin, black pepper, fennel, ginger, coconut and, of course, chili). The restaurant itself is charmingly tiny, if not charming in decor or upkeep. The food is home-cooked in style, reliable, and cheap. The coconut rice called *nasi lemak,* a kind of blue-plate special found all over the Malay peninsula, is a good bet and bargain. *$20. Licensed.*

Palayok
2717 E. Hastings St. 251-6769

This modest restaurant is a solid introduction to the cuisine of the Philippines. Begin with a bottle of San Miguel dark beer and the delicious garlic peanuts. *Ihaw-ihaw* are barbecued dishes—skewered pork that is superb, tasting both of Chinese barbecued pork and Indian tandoor kebabs. Crispy *pata* with *lechon* sauce is pork hocks with liver sauce; picture a plate of crackling with bits of roasted meat and a tart, not liverish sauce—terrific! *Kare kare* (beef with green beans, Japanese eggplant and a mild peanut gravy) is bland until you wake it up with the accompanying ferociously fishy shrimp paste. On some weekend nights, expect live, Wayne Newton-style entertainment. *$30. Licensed.*

Pho Hoang
238 E. Georgia St. 682-5666

It's hard to distinguish among the countless cafes specializing in the Vietnamese beef soup *pho* that have sprung up in Vancouver. This place serves some of the better *pho* in the pack. The broth, which varies subtly from one restaurant to the next, is exceptionally beefy here. *Pho tai* is the version with blood-rare meat. (Wonderful!) Order iced coffee with milk—a terrific caffeine high—but be sure to stir it up before you add the ice. *$6 per person. Licensed.*

Pho Van
220-633 Main St. 682-7844

There are nineteen versions of beef soup, served in giant bowls, every one a convincing argument that the world's best soups have Asian origins. All combine beef, well-done brisket, well-done flank, soft tendon, tripe, beef balls and/or "fat crispy" thrown into the same delicious, slightly sweet, beefy broth. A large plate of earthy-tasting, exceedingly fresh bean sprouts comes with it, and you add these and fresh basil and green chilies to your bowl as you like. A big place, always busy: chef Van Nguyen sells about 180 gallons of this mighty, restorative broth every day. *$12. Licensed.*

Rumah Bali
2420 Main St. 872-2908

This is a long-time Indonesian restaurant refurbished and reopened by new owners. The menu is ambitious—the dinner menu includes not only a twelve-dish, $17.25 *rijsttafel* but a whole range of regional specialties such as *pepesan ikan* (fish baked in banana leaf), *ayam belado chili* (padang-style chicken) and *laksa* (a rich coconut-milk soup with chicken, eggs and noodles). Sauces are sometimes a bit thin, some spicing a bit scant—not quite the rich deep food of great Indonesian cooking. The *gado gado* (salad with peanut sauce) was delicious, however, and the shrimp crackers and *chili sambal* (chili condiment) were perfect. *$40. Licensed.*

Tea and Silk
455 W. Broadway. 872-8866
2767 Commercial Dr. 872-1688

Tea And Silk presents a gastronomical globetrot—with the menu your Fodor's—in a tropical room that vaguely evokes a rendezvous with Greenstreet, Lorre and Bogart. The cuisines of eight southeast Asian nations are written into the menu. Just for starters: Vietnamese *cha gio* (fried spring rolls), Japanese *gyoza* (fried dumplings), Malaysian *acar ketimur* (cucumber salad), Chinese deep-fried wonton and Thai salad. Main courses run from Indian *vindaloo* curry to *bulcogi,* the sake-and-garlic-marinated and charcoal-grilled beef of Korea. The food is an exceptional bargain, with appetizers less than $4 and mains around $8. They do takeout. *$25. Licensed only at the Broadway location.*

ALPHABETICAL INDEX

Adega 15
Aki 57
Alma Street Cafe 68
The Amorous Oyster 84
Arirang House 90
Ashiana 34

Bangkok House 91
Barbara-Jo's 69
Beach Side Cafe 69
Bianco Nero 43
Bishop's 66
Bodai Vegetarian Restaurant 7
Bud's Halibut and Chips 85

Cafe de Paris 22
Cafe Il Nido 44
The Cannery 84
Cha Cha Cha 63
Chartwell 14
Chesa 16
Chez Thierry 25
Chilli House 8
CinCin 16

Dar Lebanon 36
Delilah's 71
Did's Pizza 79
Dynasty 2

Earl's 72
Elissar 37
El Mariachi 62
English Bay Cafe 73
Ezogiku Noodle Cafe 58

Five Sails 73
Flying Wedge 78
Fortune House 4

Hamburger Mary's 30
Harpo's 74
Hon's 9
Hoshi 54

Il Barino 40
Il Giardino 41

Joe Fortes 67

Kirin 6
Kitto 58
Koko 59
Kyocha Ya 59

Landmark Hot Pot House 9
Las Margaritas 63
La Toque Blanche 26
Le Club 28
Le Coq D'Or 22
Le Crocodile 24
Le Gavroche 26
Lombardo's 78

Mescalero 74
Milestones 30
Mocha Cafe 75
Monterey Lounge and Grill 75
Montri's 91
Moutai Mandarin 10

Napoli Restaurant 45
Natraj 34
Nonya Baba 92
Noodle Express 60
Nyala 37

The Only Seafood Cafe 85

Pajo's 86
Palayok 92

Park Lock 10
Passionate Pizza 79
Pepitas 64
Phnom Penh 88
Pho Hoang 93
Pho Van 93
Piccolo Mondo 45
Pink Pearl 11
Pizza Rico's 80

Raga 38
Raintree 67
Raku 55
Red Robin 31
Rubina Tandoori 35
Rumah Bali 94

Salmon House on the Hill 86
Saltimbocca 46
Salute 47
Santos Tapas 17
Sawasdee 88
Settebello 47
Slice of Gourmet 80
Sophie's Cosmic Cafe 76
Splendido 48

Tea and Silk 94
Tojo's 56

Umberto Al Porto 49

Vassilis 17
Viet Nam Cuisine 89
Villa del Lupo 42

William Tell 18

Zefferelli's 50
Zeppo's Trattoria 50

INDEX BY AREA

CHINATOWN AND NEARBY

Bodai Vegetarian Restaurant 7
Hon's 9
Hoshi 54
The Only Seafood Cafe 85
Park Lock 10
Pho Hoang 93
Pho Van 93
Phnom Penh 88
Viet Nam Cuisine 89

DOWNTOWN

Bianco Nero 43
Bud's Halibut and Chips 85
Cafe de Paris 22
Cafe Il Nido 44
Chartwell 14
Chez Thierry 25
CinCin 16
Dar Lebanon 36
Delilah's 71
Did's Pizza 79
Dynasty 2
Earl's 72
El Mariachi 62
English Bay Cafe 73
Ezogiku Noodle Cafe 58
Five Sails 73
Flying Wedge 78
Hamburger Mary's 30
Harpo's 74
Il Barino 40
Il Giardino 41
Joe Fortes 67
Kirin 6
Kitto 58
Kyocha Ya 59
Las Margaritas 63
Le Club 28
Le Crocodile 24
Le Gavroche 26
Mescalero 74
Milestones 30
Monterey Lounge and Grill 75
Moutai Mandarin 10
Nonya Baba 92
Noodle Express 60
Pepitas 64
Piccolo Mondo 45
Pizza Rico's 80
Red Robin 31
Raintree 67
Settebello 47
Slice of Gourmet 80
Splendido 48
Villa del Lupo 42
William Tell 18
Zefferelli's 50

EAST SIDE (Main St. and east)

Adega 15
Bangkok House 91
The Cannery 84
Chilli House 8
Koko 59
Lombardo's 78
Napoli Restaurant 45
Palayok 92
Pink Pearl 11
Rumah Bali 94
Santos Tapas 17

Sawasdee 88
Tea and Silk 94

GASTOWN AND NEARBY

Aki 57
Umberto Al Porto 49

HEART OF VANCOUVER (Fraser River to False Creek, Granville St. to Fraser St.)

Amorous Oyster 84
Arirang House 90
Ashiana 34
Barbara-Jo's 69
Dar Lebanon 36
Earl's 72
Fortune House 4
Kirin 6
Landmark Hot Pot House 9
Natraj 34
Passionate Pizza 79
Red Robin 31
Raga 38
Rubina Tandoori 35
Tea and Silk 94
Tojo's 56

NORTH SHORE

Beach Side Cafe 69
Chesa 16
Earl's 72
La Toque Blanche 26
Red Robin 31
Salmon House on the Hill 58
Salute 47

ODD ONES OUT

Earl's 72
Milestones 30
Pajo's 86
Red Robin 31

WEST SIDE

Alma Street Cafe 68
Bishop's 66
Cha Cha Cha 63
Earl's 72
Elissar 37
Flying Wedge 78
Las Margaritas 63
Le Coq D'Or 22
Milestones 30
Mocha Cafe 75
Montri's 91
Nyala 37
Raku 55
Saltimbocca 46
Sophie's Cosmic Cafe 76
Vassilis 17
Zeppo's Trattoria 50

INDEX BY PRICE

UP TO $20

Bud's Halibut and Chips 85
Chilli House 8
Dar Lebanon 36
Did's Pizza 79
Ezogiku Noodle Cafe 58
Flying Wedge 78
Hamburger Mary's 30
Harpo's 74
Hon's 9
Milestones 30
Nonya Baba 92
Noodle Express 60
Pajo's 86
Park Lock 10
Passionate Pizza 79
Pho Hoang 93
Pho Van 93
Pizza Rico's 80
Red Robin 31
Slice of Gourmet 80
Viet Nam Cuisine 89

$21 TO $40

Adega 15
Aki 57
Arirang House 90
Ashiana 34
Bangkok House 91
Bodai Vegetarian Restaurant 7
Cha Cha Cha 63
Earl's 72
El Mariachi 62
Elissar 37
Kitto 58
Kyocha Ya 59
Las Margaritas 63
Lombardo's 78
Montri's 91
Moutai Mandarin 10
Natraj 34
Nyala 37
The Only Seafood Cafe 85
Palayok 92
Pepitas 64
Phnom Penh 88
Pink Pearl 11
Raga 38
Rumah Bali 94
Salute 47
Santos Tapas 17
Sawasdee 88
Sophie's Cosmic Cafe 76
Tea and Silk 94
Vassilis 17

$41 TO $60

Alma Street Cafe 68
The Amorous Oyster 84
Barbara-Jo's 69
Beach Side Cafe 69
Bianco Nero 43
Cafe de Paris 22
Cafe Il Nido 44
The Cannery 84
Chesa 16
Delilah's 71
Dynasty 2
Fortune House 4
Joe Fortes 67
Koko 59
La Toque Blanche 26

Landmark Hot Pot House 9
Le Coq D'Or 22
Le Crocodile 24
Mocha Cafe 75
Monterey Lounge and Grill 75
Napoli Restaurant 45
Raintree 67
Raku 55
Rubina Tandoori 35
Salmon House on the Hill 86
Saltimbocca 46
Settebello 47
Splendido 48
Umberto Al Porto 49
Villa del Lupo 42
Zefferelli's 50
Zeppo's Trattoria 50

$61 AND UP

Bishop's 66
Chartwell 14
Chez Thierry 25
CinCin 16
English Bay Cafe 73
Five Sails 73
Hoshi 54
Il Barino 40
Il Giardino 41
Kirin 6
Le Club 28
Le Gavroche 26
Mescalero 74
Piccolo Mondo 45
Tojo's 56
William Tell 18